Upton Sinclair's THE JUNGLE

A Critical Commentary

by Walter James Miller

Professor of English
New York University

MONARCH
PRESS

Contents

Note to Student and Teacher

This monograph is a study aid for students of both history and literature.

The main function of this Monarch Note is to provide critical commentary and sociopolitical background information upon Upton Sinclair's classic novel, *The Jungle*. Basic assumptions of author and publisher are that (1) students of literature will use this work as a supplement to—not a substitute for—the original text and (2) students of history will use it as a rich secondary source.

The summaries of the story given here are working summaries—that is, they provide just enough reminder of the contents of *The Jungle* to substantiate the ongoing critical discussion and make it self-evident and to relate the plot to actual historical circumstances.

Teachers of literature will find this note helpful because it provides in-depth materials for considering Sinclair's sources, his Zolaist approach to his materials, his construction of a plot, his characterization, his style, his critical reputation.

Teachers of history will find here clues for making the tie-in between the political and cultural aspects of Sinclair's work: for example, his conversion of historical fact into fictional format, the exact nature and results of his "muckraking," his influence on Theodore Roosevelt and Congress.

THE JUNGLE:
Its Place in American History and Literature

DUAL FAME OF *THE JUNGLE*

Few works of fiction leave their stamp on political as well as literary history. In this connection, an American might think of Harriet Beecher Stowe's *Uncle Tom's Cabin*. In its serial appearance in a magazine (1851), in its publication as a book (1852), and in its long run as a stage play, *Uncle Tom's Cabin* stirred America's conscience, helping to bring about the abolition of slavery. A European would think of Ivan Turgenev's *A Sportsman's Notebook* (1852), which so dramatized the plight of Russian peasants that it induced Tsar Alexander II to emancipate the serfs.

And in discussing fiction that has achieved such double impact, both Europeans and Americans would think also of Upton Sinclair's *The Jungle*. A literary sensation in both its serialized version (1905) and its book version (1906), this novel has exerted tremendous influence on American life. Historians regard the exposés contained in *The Jungle* as one of the main reasons that President Theodore Roosevelt — and the public — pressured Congress into passing radical, landmark legislation: the Pure Food and Drug Act and a new Meat Inspection Act (1906). And President Lyndon Johnson recognized Upton Sinclair as one of the long-range forces behind the passage of the Wholesome Meat Act (1967).

1

REASONS FOR FAME

1. If we try to list the reasons why *The Jungle* has become a classic, we could start by noting that it is one of the world's best examples of how fiction can be functional: Art can serve specific human needs; it can do something political.

2. Literary historians also see *The Jungle* as one of the world's best literary expressions of passionate indignation over man's inhumanity to man.

3. *The Jungle* is one of the earliest, most successful examples of the use of Zolaist techniques by an American writer.

4. *The Jungle* is still one of those rare works in American fiction that can be called working-class novels. This fact is surprising in a country that boasts of its democracy, its pluralism, its equal treatment of all classes. (But how often have you seen a serious movie or teleplay about the problems of the working class?) In this respect *The Jungle* rates with such books as John Steinbeck's *Grapes of Wrath*.

5. For reasons given in No. 3 and No. 4., *The Jungle* is credited with helping to weaken the "genteel tradition" in American literature, thus helping to broaden the scope of subject matter and approach permitted to the author.

6. *The Jungle* also ranks high as one of America's literary ambassadors to the world. When readers outside the United States think of American literature, they think of James Fenimore Cooper, who introduced them to the Indian and the frontiersman; of Walt Whitman and Mark Twain, who developed uniquely American styles in poetry and prose, respectively; of Jack London, Upton Sinclair, Joseph Heller, and Kurt Vonnegut — who are widely translated and who show the world how American writers are free to criticize, and therefore perpetuate, the American way.

7. *The Jungle* has exerted a powerful influence on literary and public figures. The novelist F. Scott Fitzgerald said of his generation that *The Jungle* was "on our shelves before John Steinbeck ate the grapes of wrath." The "Beat Generation" poet Allen Ginsberg, the novelist Norman Mailer, the writer and Senator Daniel Patrick Moynihan, the television personality Walter Cronkite, the philosopher Herbert Marcuse all

have seen *The Jungle* as a landmark in their personal development.

For these and other reasons as we shall soon discover, Sinclair's 1906 novel is universally regarded as a classic.

Upton Sinclair, Theodore Roosevelt, and Lyndon Johnson

The Jungle reflects not only the American scene of Sinclair's young manhood but also many of his own life circumstances. It becomes important to view the novel in terms of both his life and his times.

SINCLAIR: BEFORE *THE JUNGLE*

Sinclair's early life gave him bitter first-hand knowledge of extreme differences between rich and poor. His father, Upton Senior, came of a long line of Virginia aristocrats but was himself reduced to economic hardship. The novelist's mother, on the other hand, came from the rising, wealthy Harden family of Maryland. And so Upton Sinclair, Jr., born in Baltimore in 1878, grew up experiencing this strange alternation: after his father's work took them to New York, the boy would spend most of his time in shabby rooming houses, but he would spend his holidays in the affluent home of his grandfather Harden. He literally shuttled back and forth from cheap food, bedbugs, anxiety over his father's alcoholism and economic plight, to a lavish diet, wholesome environment, cheerful comfort among the Hardens.

Determined to support himself as soon as possible, Upton Junior began his writing career as a college student. Before he was graduated from the City College of New York in 1897, he had already sold many jokes and stories to newspapers and magazines. By the time he left graduate study at Columbia University in 1900, he had published some ninety stories for boys in Street and Smith pulp magazines like *Army and Navy Weekly*.

Possibly what turned Sinclair to more serious literature was an unorthodox religious experience. From his friendship with a

4

young Episcopalian minister, Sinclair acquired a passionate devotion to moral and social justice. The Reverend W. W. Moir took the Gospels so seriously that he taught his disciples that a rich man had no chance of going to Heaven. When Moir gave Sinclair some theological works to read, Sinclair found them so contradictory in their reasoning that he lost faith in orthodox religion, but for the rest of his life he did believe in the moral teachings of Jesus. From this point on his writing became highly serious, antimaterialistic, and idealistic.

In 1900, the year of his first marriage, he wrote his first "artistic" novel, *Springtime and Harvest*, later republished as *King Midas*. None of his early books — like *The Journal of Arthur Stirling* (1903) or *Prince Hagen* (1903) — brought him either the fame or the money he so desperately needed. He and his wife and their infant son David lived for a while in a tent and even spent one fierce winter in a flimsy cabin in the New Jersey woods. But then his second novel, *Manassas* (1904), which was about the Civil War, led him to the chance of a lifetime.

HISTORY OF *THE JUNGLE*

Meat Cutters' strike. In 1904, the Amalgamated Meat Cutters, with 56,000 members, demanded that the "Beef Trust" — Armour, Cudahy, Swift, and other packers — grant a uniform wage to all workers in all their plants throughout the country. The packers responded with an offer of a minimum wage for workers classified as skilled. The union saw this as a trick. They thought the packers would later reclassify many skilled workers as unskilled. In July 1904, packing-house workers struck in nine cities, 20,000 of them in Chicago alone. But the Trust imported strikebreakers and when the union established picket lines, the press reported that "violence flared." The union soon exhausted its treasury and the strike collapsed.

Upton Sinclair, who had followed the strike carefully in the newspapers, wrote a "manifesto" called "You have lost the strike, and now what are you going to do about it?" Having recently joined the Socialist Party, he sent his essay to the Socialist weekly, *Appeal to Reason*. It appeared on the front page of the September 17, 1904 edition. And after the editor of the *Appeal*, Fred D. Warren, had read *Manassas*, he made a proposal to Sinclair: You have "portrayed the struggle over chattel slavery in America, and now, why not do the same thing for wage slavery?"

Warren advanced five hundred dollars for the serial rights to such a novel. As Sinclair would later tell it in his *American Outpost* (1932), "I selected the Chicago stockyards as its scene. The recent strike had brought the subject to my thoughts . . . my . . . manifesto had put me in touch with Socialists among the stockyards workers . . . ."

Sinclair's research in Chicago. On his twenty-sixth birthday, September 20, 1904, Sinclair took a small room in Chicago's Stockyards Hotel. For seven weeks he observed the life of the "wage slaves of the Beef Trust," as he called them: "I sat at night in the homes of the workers . . . and they told me their stories . . . and I made notes. In the daytime I would wander about the yards, and my friends would risk their jobs to show me what I wanted to see. I . . . found that by the simple device of carrying a dinner-pail I could go anywhere."

He also talked with lawyers, doctors, dentists, nurses, policemen, politicians, and real estate agents, and when he was "in doubt about the significance" of his material, he consulted Adolph Smith, Chicago correspondent for the *Lancet*, the British medical journal. Smith had made extensive studies of abattoirs and packing plants the world over. "These [Chicago plants] are not packing plants at all," Sinclair quotes Smith as having said; "these are packing-boxes crammed with wage-slaves."

What Sinclair discovered. Putting all his research together, Sinclair now had this picture of Chicago working-class life: Men, women, and children were forced to work at a furious pace, eleven or more hours a day, in cold, damp, unsanitary conditions, under the artificial stimulus of a "speed-up" system. Employers assumed no serious responsibility for injuries suffered on even the most dangerous jobs. Female employees were sexually harassed by bosses. When workers had organized to seek redress of their grievances, their union had been infiltrated by labor spies; when they had gone out on strike, the packers had used illegal methods to break the strike.

Even more sensational, so far as the welfare of the general

public was concerned, were Sinclair's discoveries about the condition of the meat packed and sold by the Beef Trust. The packers canned diseased meat and even carrion; they used chemicals to doctor spoiled meat; they swept refuse and even rats, rat dung, and rat poison into the meat vats. They duped or bribed the government inspectors who were supposedly on duty to prevent such practices.

Bribing inside the plants was simply a small part of a vast system of political graft and corruption that ruled Chicago. Illiterate immigrants were prematurely naturalized, through their employers' influence, and paid to vote as directed not once but many times. Public works were under "boss rule"; the police, the packers, and organized crime worked hand-in-hand.

Sinclair's characters. Sinclair now had his setting and his overall situation. But he could not decide on his specific characters until one Sunday when he happened to stumble on a Lithuanian wedding feast in the back room of a saloon. The bride and groom and their relatives were all recent immigrants who worked in the stockyards and allied industries. The novelist spent eight hours observing their supper and dancing. This scene actually gave Sinclair his opening chapter and many of his characters.

On his last day in Chicago — Election Day, 1904 — Sinclair delivered a speech at a mass meeting in favor of the Socialist candidate, Eugene V. Debs. Later, he would use this speech in the closing chapter of *The Jungle*.

Writing The Jungle. Back home, Sinclair borrowed a thousand dollars from a clergyman to make the down payment on a Jersey farm with an eight-room house. On the same plot of land he set up an eight-by-ten-foot shack in which he could do his writing.

On Christmas Day, 1904, Sinclair began the novel. "I wrote with tears and anguish," he tells us in *Outpost*: "Externally, the story had to do with a family of stockyards workers, but internally it was the story of my own family. Did I wish to know how the poor suffered in the winter time in Chicago? I had only to recall the previous winter in the cabin, when we had only cotton blankets, and had put rugs on top of us, and cowered shivering in our . . . beds. It was the same with hunger, with illness, with fear."

Ona, as he called the young Lithuanian bride in *The Jungle*, was modeled on Meta, the novelist's own wife. "Our little boy was down with pneumonia that winter, and nearly died, and the grief of that went into the book."

Serialization of The Jungle. Two months later, the first installment appeared in the February 25, 1905 issue of the *Appeal to Reason*. Published in Girard, Kansas, this four-page sheet devoted its entire first page and much of its inside pages to the opening chapter. The March 4 issue carried no installment because the staff wanted to give new subscribers a chance to catch up on the novel. "As the story unfolds," the editor promised, "you will be filled with wonder at the simple realism of Comrade Sinclair's style." Serialization resumed March 11 and continued until November 4, 1905, when the *Appeal* announced that the reader could "obtain the balance of the installments" in a "special edition" by simply addressing a post card to the editors.

When Sinclair had completed the manuscript in September 1905, he sent a copy to George Brett, his editor at Macmillan, who had given him a five-hundred-dollar advance after reading the first few chapters. But now Brett wanted "some of the painful details cut out" because, as Sinclair would recall in his introduction to the 1946 edition, "nothing so horrible had ever been published in America — at least not by a respectable concern." Even the well-known crusading author Lincoln Steffens advised Sinclair to make the cuts. But Sinclair refused and the book was rejected — not only by Macmillan but also by four other publishers.

The *Appeal* now urged its readers to subsidize the book by ordering copies and paying in advance (a classical method used by Alexander Pope and Dr. Samuel Johnson to finance some of their works). The famous novelist Jack London wrote a rousing "manifesto," promising that "what *Uncle Tom's Cabin* did for black slaves, *The Jungle* had a large chance to do for the white slaves. . . ." Twelve thousand orders poured in, and the book was set up in type in a special "Sustainer's Edition."

Doubleday's two investigations. At this point, Doubleday, Page and Company offered to publish a commercial edition if they could verify the novel's "essential truth." Walter Page sent the galley proofs of *The Jungle* to James Keeley, managing editor of *The Chicago Tribune,* who sent back a thirty-two-page report declaring that "everything in the book was false." Sinclair persuaded Page to send two of his own representatives to Chicago. The first, a lawyer, met a publicity agent at Armour's, who said smugly: "*The Jungle?* Oh yes, I know that book. I read the proofs of it, and prepared a thirty-two-page report for James Keeley of the *Tribune.*"

The second representative, Doubleday editor I. F. Marcosson, reported that *The Jungle* contained no serious misstatements; if anything, the book was an understatement. "I was able to get a Meat Inspector's Badge," Marcosson said, "which gave me access to the secret confines of the meat empire. Day and night I prowled over its foul-smelling domain and I was able to see with my own eyes much that Sinclair had never even heard about."

On January 27, 1906, *The New York Times Book Review* noted that the lawyer's report had upheld Sinclair and so the book would be published on February 15. But on February 17, the *Book Review* announced a postponement until February 26.

The Times *versus the public.* Less than a week after the Doubleday edition appeared, the *Book Review* responded with a full-page critique — but on page 128! The critic — anonymous, as was then often the case in reviewing — explained the need for such full treatment. "Inasmuch as Mr. Upton Sinclair's co-workers in the field of Socialistic propaganda have acclaimed his book as 'a great book' . . . it becomes the plain duty of the reviewer to examine *The Jungle* with a candid and open mind, that its quality as literature and its efficiency as polemic may be fairly appraised."

While he found the novel "in many ways a brilliant study of the great Chicago industries," he decided on balance that it failed both as literature and as polemic (see Chapter VI, "Critical Reputation," for more details). Some libraries put *The Jungle* on limited circulation because of its "immorality."

But such negative reactions seem to have been isolated cries drowned out by a general public approval. The *New York Evening World* — a crusading newapaper more in sympathy with Sinclair's position — soon declared: "Not since Byron awoke one morning to find himself famous has there been such an example of worldwide celebrity won in a day by a book as has come to

Upton Sinclair." And the famous British novelist, H.G. Wells, on a visit to America, had been asked to look up a young writer believed to be starving in New York. Instead Wells found Sinclair "not merely a wealthy man," as I.O. Evans has put it, "but the centre of the world's attention."

Sinclair versus Armour. Meanwhile, J. Ogden Armour spent "three days and nights with his lawyers, avowing his determination to have the author of that book indicted for criminal libel." According to Mary Craig Sinclair, the novelist's second wife, Armour's lawyers forced him to "realize that they couldn't face the evidence" that crusaders like Sinclair "might rake up."

But Armour — or, as Robert Downs says, Armour's ghost writers — had been running a series of articles in the *Saturday Evening Post*. In the sixth article, Mr. Armour took cognizance of *The Jungle*:

> Strangely enough, in view of its vital importance, . . . government inspection has been the subject of endless misrepresentation — of *ignorantly or maliciously false statements.* The public has been told that meat animals and carcasses condemned as diseased are afterward secretly made use of by the packers and sold to the public for food in the form of both dressed meats and canned meats . . . . I repeat: In Armour and Co.'s business *not one atom of any condemned animal or carcass finds its way, directly or indirectly, into any food product or food ingredient.* [italics Armour's]

Circulation of the *Post* was 655,772 at that time, and so Sinclair had good reason to "boil." The very day he read this article, Sinclair would recall later in *Outpost*, "I . . . sat down and wrote all through the night, and next morning had an eight-thousand-word magazine article . . . ." He took the next train to New York and read the manuscript aloud to the assembled editors of *Everybody's Magazine*, which "had just electrified the country with Tom Lawson's exposure of Wall Street methods." They bought the article on the spot for eight hundred dollars, "stopped the presses on which the May issue was being printed, and took out a story to make room" for Sinclair's rebuttal of Armour.

"The Condemned Meat Industry: A Reply to Mr. J. Ogden Armour" appeared on the newsstands on April 20, 1906. Sinclair reviewed the "embalmed beef scandal" of the Spanish-American

War, "when the whole country was convulsed . . . over the reve-
lation made by soldiers . . . concerning the quality of meat which
Armour and Co. had furnished to the troops." Sinclair then produced an affidavit, notarized in New York, in which Thomas F.
Dolan, a one-eyed Irish-American foreman on Armour's killing
beds, had sworn that condemned carcasses, thrown into tanks to
be destroyed, were regularly removed at the bottom of the tanks
and then sold in the city as dressed meat. Sinclair went on to tell
how Armour had offered Dolan five thousand dollars to keep
quiet, how Dolan "took the five new crisp one thousand dollar
bills and deposited them in the bank, to be held in trust for the
education of his children," and then gave out the story to the
New York Evening Journal. This was the headline:

ARMOUR PAYS $5000 FOR A GOLD BRICK IN BOSTON!

Sinclair then reviewed the court records of many pleas of guilty
which Armour and other firms had entered to the charge of selling adulterated meat products. This piece was typical of several
articles that Sinclair published during this period (see Chapter
VII, "Selected Bibliography").

Roosevelt's mixed feelings. Meanwhile President Roosevelt
had been kept informed of all these developments by Sinclair, by
his Socialist publishers, and by his commercial publishers. During the 1905 serialization of *The Jungle*, the President's secretary received about a hundred letters a day from *Appeal*
readers. Sinclair himself sent the President a copy of the "Sustainer's Edition," and I.F. Marcosson sent T. R. a copy of the
commercial edition. Both Marcosson and Sinclair received word
from Roosevelt that he was "investigating" the charges.

As early as March 12, 1906, as a matter of fact, the President
had directed Secretary of Agriculture James Wilson to look into
the novelist's charges. Enclosing "a personal appeal from Sinclair," T.R. asked that "a first-class man . . . be appointed to
meet Sinclair." Then, in an exchange of letters with the author,
T.R. agreed that energetic action had to be taken against "arro-
gant and selfish greed on the part of the capitalist," but he
deplored the "pathetic belief" of the characters who "preach
socialism" in the last sections of *The Jungle*. Roosevelt said he
distrusted "men of hysterical temperament" but admitted that

this had little to do with the "fact that the specific evils you point out [should], if their existence be proved, and if I have the power, be eradicated."

Roosevelt's two investigations. The first commissioners sent by Secretary Wilson to Chicago apparently only inquired at the top and, according to Downs, they "were persuaded by the Beef Trust that *The Jungle* was the product of a disordered and sensation-seeking mind." Sinclair replied to Roosevelt that "having the Department of Agriculture investigate the matter" was "like having a burglar determine his own guilt." This striking analogy resulted in an invitation to lunch at the White House. On that occasion, Roosevelt said, "Mr. Sinclair, I bear no love for these gentlemen, for I ate the meat they canned for the Army in Cuba."

The President now appointed a second commission, composed of two social workers from New York, Commissioner of Labor Charles P. Neill, and Assistant Secretary of the Treasury James Bronson Reynolds. They asked Sinclair to accompany them, but instead he sent a well-known Trenton Socialist, Ella Reeve Bloor. With Bloor working through the same Socialist contacts that had helped Sinclair two years before, the Neill-Reynolds commission obtained evidence of practically everything charged in *The Jungle*. The main exception was that they could find no evidence of any man having fallen into a vat and having gone out into the world as canned lard. They submitted their full report to the President.

Roosevelt pressures Congress. The President's old friend, Senator Albert Beveridge of Indiana, had long been telling Roosevelt about the "nauseous conditions" in the stockyards and packing houses. He had framed and introduced a Meat Inspection Bill, but on May 25, 1906, he unexpectedly offered it as an amendment to the Agricultural Appropriations Bill. The *New York Times* first-page account of his maneuver gave Sinclair full credit:

WASHINGTON, May 25. — The Senate today furnished another surprise in the line of radical legislation by passing the Beveridge Meat Inspection bill. Fifteen minutes before it was passed not a Senator would have admitted that the bill had a ghost of a chance to become a law. . . . Its passage is the direct consequence of the disclosures made in Upton Sinclair's novel, "The Jungle."

. . . There were possibly twenty Senators present when the amendment was offered, but in the number were three or four to whom the President had said within the last few days that he would send to Congress and make public the special report by . . . Neill . . . and . . . Reynolds, on the condition of things in Chicago unless something were done to correct the evils complained of in the conduct of the packing business . . .

The disclosures made in . . . "The Jungle," which led to the passage of the measure, astounded President Roosevelt when he read the book. He could not believe they had any foundation in truth. . . . He sent Mr. Sinclair an invitation to come to Washington and tell him how he got his information.

The President saw that he was dealing with a man who knew what he was talking about, and he told Labor Commissioner Neill and Assistant Secretary of the Treasury Reynolds to go to Chicago . . . it is said they found Sinclair had not exaggerated the actual conditions. Their report has been in the hands of the President for several days and would have been sent to Congress had not the Beveridge bill been passed.

The House Agriculture Committee, nevertheless, dragged its feet.

Chairman James Wadsworth, known as a partisan of the packers, came up with many new amendments that would have emasculated the Beveridge bill. For example, Wadsworth wanted a clause that would allow the packers to appeal the inspectors' rulings in the court and hence, in the words of W.H. Harbaugh, "evade the law by endless litigation." T.R. was enraged but apparently still hesitated to send the Neill-Reynolds report to the House.

Sinclair himself claims credit for forcing the release of the report. "With the tacit consent of the commission, I put *The New York Times* onto the track of . . . Mrs. Bloor . . . I moved up to New York and opened an amateur publicity office . . . with two secretaries working overtime. I gave interviews and wrote statements for the press until I was dizzy," he writes in *Outpost*.

The *Times* reflects Sinclair's campaign. It ran page-one stories, crediting and quoting Sinclair, every day from May 26 to May 30. Three times, on its editorial page during that week, the *Times* demanded release of the Neill-Reynolds document.

"So," says Sinclair, "Roosevelt had to publish the report, and the truth was out."

As Roosevelt had predicted, "confirmation of the charges made in Sinclair's novel had a devastating impact upon the packing industry's sales," says Harbaugh. Meat lobbyists who had attacked the Beveridge amendment as "socialistic" and "unconstitutional" now reversed themselves, because now they were eager to get the government's stamp of approval on their products and regain their market, especially in Europe.

After further debate, both the Pure Food and Drug Act and the Beef Inspection Act were passed, less than six months after *The Jungle* had appeared in book form.

Roosevelt snubs "muckraker" Sinclair. Ironically, the President gave more credit to Beveridge than to Sinclair, and the novelist felt that his purposes had miscarried, his efforts been deflected. After the President signed the agricultural bill, he gave the pen he had used to Beveridge. "You were the man who first called my attention to abuses in the packing houses," Roosevelt wrote to Beveridge. But to Sinclair, the President gave nothing, nor did he even mention Sinclair in his autobiography.

Actually, Sinclair should not have been surprised by Roosevelt's snub. For on April 14, 1906, the President had delivered a speech complaining that some political writers — whom he dubbed "muckrakers" — were going too far in their exposés. (See "Overview of *The Jungle*: Story, Themes, Techniques.") Apparently, Roosevelt and Beveridge had simply used Sinclair; they exploited the sensation created by *The Jungle* as their big chance to take steps they had been planning for some time. And Roosevelt's failure to acknowledge Sinclair's role may have reflected his desire not to be seen as endorsing the "hysterical" Socialist passages in the novel.

Sinclair had other reasons for feeling let down. He had written *The Jungle*, as we have seen, mainly to attract attention to the plight of the American workingman. Less than a dozen pages of his novel deal with processing of impure food. Most of the book is about the exploitation of labor. Yet the novel succeeded immediately, and almost exclusively, in arousing the country to the need for pure food legislation.

In the introduction to his 1946 edition of *The Jungle*, Sinclair summed up his feelings in his most famous remark: "I aimed at the public's heart, and by accident I hit it in the stomach." In his *Outpost*, he says: "I am supposed to have helped clean up the yards and improve the country's meat supply — though this is mostly delusion. But nobody even pretends . . . that I improved the condition of the stockyards workers." (Students interested in following up on these questions should start with works by Harvey Swados and William Bloodworth listed in the selected bibliography.)

SINCLAIR: AFTER *THE JUNGLE*

Only twenty-eight when *The Jungle* established his fame, Upton Sinclair was a politically active writer for the next sixty-two years. At times he lived in experimental communes. Divorced from Meta Fuller in 1912, he married Mary Craig Kimbrough and moved to California in 1914. His sixteenth major work, *King Coal* (1917), a novel dealing with labor problems in the coal mines of Colorado, contained an introduction by the famous Danish critic, Georg Brandes.

After his thirty-fifth major book, including outstanding novels like *Oil!* and *Boston*, he won the 1934 Democratic Party primary for governor in California. His famous EPIC campaign — "End Poverty in California" — nearly won him the election. In 1940 he began a notable experiment in "contemporary historical fiction." By 1953, he had published eleven novels about Lanny Budd, a character who manages to figure in, or at least witness, almost every crucial historical event from 1919 to 1949. One novel in this series, *Dragon's Teeth* (1942), covering Hitler's rise to power, won the Pulitzer Prize; and another, *A World to Win* (1946), about American developments in 1940 – 1942, sold more than seven hundred thousand copies. When Sinclair published his autobiography (an updating of *Outpost*) in 1962 (the year also of his third marriage), it was his sixtieth major work. His total output, which runs to eighty volumes, includes nonfiction and drama as well as fiction.

Lyndon Johnson and Sinclair. On December 16, 1967, Sinclair again made the first page of *The New York Times*:

JOHNSON WELCOMES UPTON SINCLAIR, 89,
AT MEAT BILL SIGNING

As Max Frankel described the ceremony, the President had invited the novelist to "witness the signing of the Wholesome Meat Act," which would gradually plug loopholes left by the first Federal meat inspection law: "Mr. Sinclair . . . helped enact that law as a politician . . . and . . . through his exposure of unsanitary conditions in the meat industry in a book 'The Jungle' in 1906."

"In a wheelchair, attended by a nurse, daughter, and son-in-law, Mr. Sinclair . . . stood with assistance through a special tribute to his own efforts at the start of the century and shook hands warmly after Mr. Johnson gave him one of the pens used in the signing."

And so President Johnson had carefully arranged to give Upton Sinclair the official recognition that an earlier president had deprived him of. This ceremony occurred just eleven months before Sinclair, an author admired the world over, died in November 1968.

Overview of THE JUNGLE:
Story, Themes, Techniques

Before we embark on a chapter-by-chapter analysis of *The Jungle*, it will be helpful to define our critical terms and establish an overview of Sinclair's story, his themes, and the techniques he used to achieve his effects.

STORY AND PLOT

In analyzing fiction, we find it valuable to distinguish between story and plot. *Story is the chronological order in which the events occurred. Plot is the nonchronological order in which the author has chosen to reveal those events.*

To understand Sinclair's narrative techniques, then, let us review first the basic *story* and then the *plot* he designed to unfold that story.

STORY: CHRONOLOGICAL

In the late 1890s, Jurgis Rudkus, his father Antanas, his fiancée Ona, her stepmother Elzbieta, and her family live in the Lithuanian forest. Basically they live well, eating natural foods, working out-of-doors, residing in sturdy cabins, enjoying a communal village life. But they are oppressed and cheated by the upper classes. Into their village come agents from Chicago, telling them that in America, high-paying jobs are waiting for immigrants. In America everyone is "equal" and can do as he pleases.

As a matter of fact, they hear that one man from their village, Jokubas, has made a fortune in the Chicago stockyards.

The two families work hard, save money, embark for America — six adults, six children. In New York they are cheated by uniformed officials. In Chicago they find Jokubas running a debt-ridden delicatessen. The rooming house he takes them to is the most crowded, most unhealthful place they have ever seen. But Jurgis, impressed by American technology, believes that if he works hard and does as he is told, he will achieve security for his family.

Initial successes. Jurgis, Elzbieta's brother Jonas, Ona's cousin Marija, and finally Grandfather Antanas all get jobs in the packing plants. They sign a mortgage and move into a "new" house. They are happy "feathering their nest" and planning for the big wedding.

Disillusionment. But soon they suffer disenchantment, learning first-hand about oppressive, dangerous conditions in the plants, about the processing of dangerously impure meats, and about a system of graft that pervades both industrial management and city government. They learn that they have been conned by a real estate agent who sells old homes as new and has concealed the real costs from them in the hope they would fail to meet their payments and be dispossessed. In despair, they send Ona and even Elzbieta's children out to work, and Jurgis accepts bribes to vote the way the bosses (industrial and political) tell him to.

Thus, when Jurgis and Ona are finally able to marry, they start out off-balance; they sink further into debt when an old Lithuanian custom for communal financing of a wedding feast fails miserably in noncommunal America.

Antanas dies of illnesses caused by his working conditions, the youngest child dies of convulsions after eating contaminated food, and Jurgis is forced to take the most hazardous, most humiliating work of all — in a fertilizer plant. Meanwhile Ona, who has borne a child, is coerced by her boss into illicit sex; unless she yields, he will fire all the wage-earners in her family. When Jurgis learns of Ona's plight, during her second pregnancy, he attacks her boss and is jailed; they all lose their jobs and are dispossessed.

After Ona dies in premature childbirth, and Jurgis' son in a street accident, Jurgis spends a summer in the country — now a tramp, now a migratory worker. Winter drives him back to Chicago where he works on tunnel construction until he breaks his arm. Forced to panhandle, he accidentally gets a hundred-dollar bill from a rich man, is cheated out of it by a bartender, goes berserk, then goes back to jail.

Illegal solutions. Disillusioned now with law and order, Jurgis drifts into crime, becoming first a mugger, then a hireling of a corrupt political machine, and finally a corrupt strikebreaker. For the first time in his life, he is financially well off. But meeting Ona's boss, he again assaults him and again is jailed. Back to begging on the streets, he discovers that Marija supports the surviving members of the family by working in a house of prostitution.

Legal solutions. One night Jurgis stumbles into a Socialist meeting. He hears a speech that sums up American working-class life as he knows it. He is converted to the Socialist mission of building, by democratic means, a society in which industry would be owned by the people at large. He gets a job as a hotel porter and helps the Socialists turn out a record vote in the 1904 Chicago election.

PLOT: NONCHRONOLOGICAL

Instead of recounting these events in their chronological order, Sinclair devises a *plot*. He begins his novel *in medias res* (in the middle of things): with the wedding feast. This major event in the lives of Jurgis and Ona gives Sinclair a perfect opportunity to introduce most of his characters, their life circumstances, and some of his main themes. Then, in Chapters 2 through 6, he uses a series of *flashbacks* to fill us in on the earlier history of the two families in Lithuania and America. In Chapter 7 he resumes the action where Chapter 1 had left off. In Chapters 7 through 31 he uses *continuous action with occasional flashbacks*, the most important being Ona's confession to Jurgis of how her illicit relation with her boss Connor had begun months before.

Sinclair's rearrangement of time and events thus gives us a perfect example of the difference between story and plot. From the author's point of view, plot is a mechanism for unfolding a story in a suspenseful, dramatic manner. From the reader's point of view, plot is the means by which he gradually pieces together the full story.

How Sinclair structures his separate chapters is best taken up later, after we have examined the themes of his novel, for Sinclair's narrative techniques prove to be determined partly by his overall message.

THEMES

As we have seen in our account of Sinclair's career, he wrote *The Jungle* with the definite intention of exposing the cruel conditions under which employees of the meat-packing industry worked and lived. But the plot he devised ultimately took his characters into so many different situations that Sinclair was able to touch on many broader questions. We can restate the final results in the form of ten major themes. There is much overlapping here; the themes are interrelated.

1. *In 1900 – 1904, industrialized America is a jungle.* The only real law is the law of the jungle: might makes right.
2. *The main problem is that the economic system fosters greed and ruthless competition as a way of life.* Greed prompts people to sell spoiled meat, engage in false advertising, pollute, bribe and be bribed.
3. *In such a system, the hired worker lives at a distinct disadvantage.* He is trapped, exploited, and cheated by employers who, in competition with other employers, must consider profits more important than people.
4. *The worker in early twentieth-century America is brutalized and stultified.* Only that part of his personality needed to perform a monotonous task is kept alive; the rest is crushed. Under these conditions, love is reduced to mere bestiality; the tender aspects of marriage and the raising of children are harshly overshadowed by the agonies of the economic struggle; and indeed, marriage itself becomes an economic trap.
5. *Equality of opportunity is a myth.* The rich have a headstart

in every area of life. The only equality is this: Americans of all classes are corrupted by crass materialism.

6. *Big Business has complete control of, but no responsibility for, the well-being of the masses.* Big Business ultimately, deviously, controls government and the courts for its own benefit. In order to foster its corruption of politics, Big Business needs and connives at crime and ultimately works in alliance with the criminal world.

7. *Capitalist democracy is therefore a fraud, a contradiction in terms.* There can be no democracy in a society controlled by one class with hereditary power.

8. *Turn-of-the-century immigrants to America were lured into a trap.* They were attracted by promises of economic well-being and political equality; instead, they were sacrificed on the altar of "progress," the generation that built industrial society for its native owners. "Here, precisely as in Russia [1904] . . . rich men owned everything."

9. *American greatness is due to exploitation.* "If we are the greatest nation the sun has ever shone upon, it would seem to be mainly because we have been able to goad wage earners to [a] pitch of frenzy."

10. *The only solution is to transfer control of the means of production from private to public ownership, through democratic processes.*

As we shall see, Sinclair's plot and other literary maneuvers were all designed to dramatize these themes.

LITERARY TECHNIQUES

When he wrote *The Jungle*, Sinclair combined several different literary approaches. He used a modified form of Naturalism, the literary approach invented by Émile Zola (1840 – 1902). Sinclair incorporated into his fiction some of the nonfiction techniques recently developed by the so-called muckrakers. And he employed most of the traditional techniques — narrative, metaphoric, symbolic, stylistic — developed by writers from Homer down to Jack London, Sinclair's contemporary.

Naturalism (Zolaism). Émile Zola believed that Charles Darwin's discoveries and methods now made it possible for the novelist to *develop fiction as a science*. The main requirement is that the novelist systematically study his characters as products of their heredity and environment. To accomplish this, Zola maintained, the writer must approach his material with scientific objectivity, scrapping all preconceptions, sentimental attachments, and moral judgments, and simply observe and record the data on his human specimens. Zola meant not selected data but *all* data: the whole truth, no matter how trivial, disgusting, impolite, or "unliterary."

The novelist must abandon the *traditional* plot, which Zola saw as a deliberate tampering with the data of life to produce a predetermined moral effect — as when novels end with virtue rewarded, evil punished, rational order brought out of chaos. Instead of contriving such a plot, the Zolaist must trace the *chain of causation*: each step in the action must proceed logically from previous conditions. Human sentiment, triumph, fate should appear as inevitable workings-out of the laws of biology.

Three Darwinist elements especially figure in Zolaism. (1) Any *change of environment* must be studied for its effects on the species: physical, social, moral. (2) The element of *chance, luck, coincidence, accident* — all of them important in Darwinian evolution — must be given a prominent role in fiction. (3) The novelist must pay special attention to *techniques of survival in the struggle for existence*.

In Zola's hands, this approach usually created characters who are simply the end product of circumstances. *A typical naturalist character does not so much grow as become progressively aware of how he is trapped by previous conditions and by nature itself*. Economics and marriage are typical traps. In falling in love and becoming married, a person falls prey first to nature's need to reproduce. Then he becomes a victim of employers who can exploit his need for money to support a family, and of business men who can cheat him all the way from selling him a flimsy house to overcharging him for a funeral.

Sinclair's modified Zolaism. Sinclair followed Zolaism so far as it served his political ends. Notebook in hand, as Zola required, he recorded exhaustive information about the life and work of laborers in Chicago. He did sufficient research into the cultural background and heredity of families of Lithuanian origin, and he used the detailed effects of their change of environment — from European forest to Chicago slum — as one of the main subjects of his story.

He has agreed with the Zolaist position that a writer must tell the complete truth, no matter how sordid. He tells us about roaches in a rooming house, rats in the meat plants, a police raid on a house of prostitution. He documents techniques repeatedly, until we know how schoolboys become newsboys, how one machine converts rods into bolts and another links sausages, how raking in garbage heaps is more profitable in winter because the food is better preserved in freezing weather. We learn how a political party can rig an election; how a family, a single man, and a prostitute budget their earnings; how professional panhandlers fake their physical conditions.

Furthermore, several crucial developments in *The Jungle* depend on sheer luck, good or bad. If the streetcars had not stopped running on a certain freezing night, Jurgis might never have discovered Ona's relation with Connor; they might have been "saved." And it was pure chance that the political meeting Jurgis took refuge in was a Socialist gathering.

Departures from Zolaism. But Sinclair departs from orthodox naturalism in three respects: (1) He makes no pretense of detachment or objectivity; he is passionately on the side of the workers and gives us precious little of the other side of the story. He does not scrap his sentimental attachments or his moral judgments: rather, he exploits them for all they're worth. (2) He rescues at least one character from the typical Zolaist fate. While Jurgis' father, wife, son, Elzbieta and her children, Marija and her lover all go down to defeat as the victims of circumstances, Jurgis manages to escape the trap. However, a case could be made for seeing Jurgis' fate as still Zolaist in this one respect: It was *chance* that led him into a good environment, the good Socialist environment that alone gave him new hope and new purpose. (3) Sinclair's ending, in any case, is not a truly Zolaist conclusion. *The Jungle* does not end in the total defeat so typical of the naturalistic novel.

Muckraking. Sinclair's novel owes almost as much to the muckrakers as it does to the Zolaists. The muckrakers were a group of nonfiction writers who investigated abuses in business and politics. Some of their best work appeared in magazines, like Charles E. Russell's articles on the Beef Trust, which ran in *Everybody's* (1905). They also produced best-selling books, like Lincoln Steffens' *The Shame of the Cities* and Ida M. Tarbell's *The History of the Standard Oil Company* (both 1904). They were dubbed "muckrakers" by President Theodore Roosevelt in a speech delivered on April 14, 1906. He likened them to a character in Bunyan's *Pilgrim's Progress* "who could look no way but downward with the muckrake in his hand . . . [and] continued to rake to himself the filth of the floor." While agreeing that many of the muckrakers' charges were justified, Roosevelt complained that some of their methods were sensational and irresponsible. They adopted his slur as a badge of honor, henceforth referring to themselves as muckrakers.

So, from the moment Sinclair set out for Chicago to document evils in the packing plants, he was a muckraker as well as a quasi-Zolaist. He was preparing further exposés for an audience already accustomed to one sensational exposé after another. In the actual writing of *The Jungle*, he was not only guided by the work of Russell and Steffens, but also used their methods. True, he cast many of his industrial and political revelations into fictional form. But he also wrote whole sections of *The Jungle* as though they were nonfiction essays, written for *McClure's*, *Collier's*, or the *New York World*.

Autobiographical documentation. In addition to using the fruits of his Zolaist notetaking and his muckraking detective work, Sinclair drew often on his own personal experiences. When he wrote in *The Jungle* about vermin in filthy mattresses, he was writing from his own experiences in the rundown hotels where his father often housed the Sinclairs. When he described Jurgis' guilt in fighting Demon Rum, he was really writing about his father's struggle with alcoholism (Upton Senior would die of *delirium tremens* just one year after *The Jungle* appeared). When Ona suffers "womb trouble" and her baby is nursed through childhood illnesses, Sinclair was using his own direct observations of the ailments of his wife and son. Even the Rudkus family's sufferings in their flimsy Chicago house in the cold of winter were based on the Sinclair family's night-long shivering in their Jersey cabin. And the political speech with which Sinclair concludes *The Jungle* was modeled on one he actually delivered in Chicago on Election night, 1904. All through the book, as Sinclair contrasts the life of rich and poor, he was drawing on his own family backgrounds: the comfortable life of his mother's relatives, the squalid life of his father.

Narrative techniques. So far we have seen that Sinclair chose to use the technique of starting his story *in medias res* (Chapter 1), filling in the earlier action with flashbacks (for example, Chapters 2 – 6, 9) which he uses again in the crisis of Chapter 15. He chose too, in his muckraking zeal, to use a blend of fictional narrative with outright nonfictional exposition.

We should comment now on his chapter design. For example, he sometimes structures a chapter on the *ebb-and-flow* pattern of his characters' fortunes and moods. A simple example is Chapter 5: In the first half, all the characters are happy in their "nest feathering." In the second, all the wage earners face a staggering series of disillusionments. In several chapters (as explained later in the chapter "Chapter-by-Chapter Analysis"), Sinclair repeats the ebb-and-flow cycle more than once.

Sometimes, his chapter design can be better described as *alternation of summary-scene-summary, or of introspection-action-introspection.* All of these devices, *ebb-and-flow, scene-summary, thinking-acting*, are variations of Sinclair's master technique of alternating the means and the moods involved in his storytelling.

Characterization. For all of his main characters but one, Sinclair uses the simple Darwinist-Zolaist approach: people are products of heredity and environment, of luck and circumstance, and especially of changes in environment. The children change first when their food changes from natural European country food to adulterated American city food; they change again when they go from the protection of home and school to the jungle of street life as newsboys. Jurgis discovers in himself long-forgotten traits when he goes from urban air to country air.

In addition to using these Zolaist emphases, Sinclair employs other characterization devices well refined by centuries of Western fiction and drama. He casts Jurgis as a *naif*: an innocent person whose struggles to learn the hard facts of life educate the reader too about what those facts are. He *contrasts* his characters so as better to bring out the distinguishing traits of each. You will find him, for example, comparing Marija with Tamoszius, with Ona, and with Jurgis. And, of course, he contrasts what a character *is* at one point in the story to what the character *becomes* in reaction to later experiences. Marija now defends propriety, later learns impropriety as a way of life. Jurgis now believes in the work ethic, later believes in jungle tactics, later in collaboration.

Although Sinclair is not especially concerned with psychology, he does indicate the internal struggles of some characters. For several chapters we see Ona in mysterious hysteria, in secret conflict over her clandestine sexual life. And Jurgis repeatedly experiences guilt feelings: over his spending family money for drink, over his first mugging, over his role as strikebreaker. Indeed his first reaction on hearing a Socialist denunciation of working-class conditions is guilt over having accepted them for so long.

In addition to developing and changing his main characters over thirty-one chapters, Sinclair proves to be good at quick thumbnail sketches of people who appear just once, like Finnergan, or twice, like Madame Haupt or Mike Scully. In some of these, Sinclair is once again using a nonfiction magazine-writer's technique, as we see in his series of succinct thumbnail sketches of Socialist leaders (Chapter 30). When we supply the real names of these Socialists, like Jack London, we discover we have something closer to biography than to fiction.

Sense appeal. When he functions more as a fiction writer than a propagandist, Sinclair excels at accurate use of sense appeal. He catches sounds that pervade an environment, like the "broom, broom" of a cello in a three-piece orchestra, or the lowing of cattle and the grunting of swine that blend to create the characteristic stockyards noise. He gives us the smells that assail the characters when Jurgis himself is called "The Stinker" during his days in the fertilizer plant. Sinclair details sights, all the way from patterns on a vest to the way smoke changes colors with waning sunlight. He is significantly weaker in representing taste and touch.

Symbolism and allegory. A *symbol* is something that stands for something larger than itself. A *sustained symbolic action*, with a surface meaning that hides another meaning, is called an *allegory*. Sinclair uses both. When Jurgis flees to the country, he bathes in a stream in a way that is clearly a ritual of baptism, and he pulls up young trees in a symbolic rehearsal for rebellion. Sinclair also uses timing for ironic symbolism: Ona's absences from home occur just before Thanksgiving and just before Christmas.

Sinclair's famous allegory in *The Jungle* is his implied parallel between hogs and human beings. The hog has "gone about his business" while "a horrid fate awaited in his pathway" and he becomes "so very human" in his protest. The irony is that Jurgis says, "I'm glad I'm not a hog." Later, his Socialist mentor assures him that the packers have used him just as they use hogs. Sinclair's hog allegory might well have provided the basis for James Agee's masterpiece, "A Mother's Tale."

Simile, metaphor, analogy. In the more poetic sections of *The Jungle*, Sinclair uses figures of speech that achieve their effect by making us experience a memorable similarity between dissimilar things. The *simile* is the most obvious, since it uses an equal sign (in the form of a *like* or an *as*) to establish the similarity. Thus, Sinclair says that when Madame Haupt walked, "she rolled like a small boat on the ocean." Elzbieta is "like the angleworm, which goes on living though cut in half." Midwives "grow thick as fleas in Packingtown."

The *metaphor* states the comparison implicitly, without an equal sign. Sinclair sees cattle going through the chutes as "a very river of death." Jurgis and Ona and Elzbieta see their hopes "buried in separate graves." Sinclair uses an *extended analogy* to develop his characters' struggle in terms of the Darwinist "survival of the fittest." Just as in winter "storms . . . strew the ground with . . . weaker branches," so the "annual harvest" of winter illness cuts down the ill-clad, ill-housed, weaker workers.

Style. Sinclair's *style* and *tone* vary tremendously. In the earlier chapters, written under less pressure, his prose is full and rich, emotional and dramatic. In the hastily written final chapters, his prose is thin, shallow, factual, sounding more like a social worker's case history than artistic fiction. In dealing with emotions, Sinclair is always better at violent drama, anger, fury, indignation. When he depicts the tenderer, more poignant human feelings, he turns trite, sentimental, inept. He is effective at humor, satire, and sarcasm, but unfortunately does not use these talents often.

Literary allusions. Another literary technique in which Sinclair ranges from strength to weakness is the use of literary allusions. He is writing "in character" when he has educated Socialists alluding to Voltaire, Frank Norris, and Nietzsche. But he diffuses and dilutes his effect when he describes the condition, reflections, and observations of illiterate characters in terms of Dante, Goethe, Francis Bacon, Oscar Wilde, and Homer — authors these people have never heard of.

Techniques combined. In our next chapter, we shall discuss numerous, detailed examples of how Sinclair combines all these techniques — Zolaism, muckraking, narrative devices, modes of characterization, sense appeal, figurative imagery, style and tone — to realize his themes and create *The Jungle.*

Chapter-by-Chapter
Textual Analysis

Title. Sinclair creates suspense with his very first words: *The Jungle.* His title connotes a wild, dark, threatening environment, an uncivilized scene of ruthless competition and violent struggle for survival. The title also invokes the concept of "the law of the jungle": that might makes right, that gentleness, innocence, virtue, and love are at the mercy of raw power.

Dedication. Most editions still carry the original dedication: "To the Workingmen of America." This reminds us that *The Jungle* was frankly offered as "proletarian literature" in a time when there was a strong "class consciousness" in America. As we have seen, the original 1905 version had run serially in the Socialist weekly, *Appeal to Reason.* When the *Appeal* announced a 1906 edition in book format, Sinclair's fellow Socialist, noted novelist Jack London, wrote a broadside proclaiming: "Here it is at last! . . . . Comrade Sinclair's book. . . . And what *Uncle Tom's Cabin* did for black slaves, *The Jungle* has a large chance to do for the white slaves of today . . . ."

Chapter 1

PLOT DEVELOPMENT

Sinclair chooses to open his story with a crowded social event that allows him rapidly to introduce many characters, their circumstances, the problems they face, the sociopolitical context of their lives.

Jurgis Rudkus and Ona Lukoszaite, Lithuanian immigrants who work in the Chicago stockyards, have just been married. We meet them at their wedding supper and dance, held in a saloon "back of the yards." Ona's cousin, Marija Bercynskas, is determined that the party proceed with due regard to Lithuanian custom. (With her devotion to the proprieties, Sinclair sets the stage for a sadly ironic development in Marija's own life later in the story.) Dede Antanas (Grandfather Anthony) makes a speech so pessimistic — his health is bad: he works in a cold, damp packinghouse — that Jokubas Szedvilas, delicatessen operator, takes over the duty of delivering happy congratulations to the newlyweds. The most dramatic, most symbolic event is the *acziavimas*, a ceremonial dance. Guests circle around the bride as one by one, the men dance with her. Teta Elzbieta — "Aunt" Elizabeth, Ona's stepmother — holds out a hat so each male dancer can meet his solemn obligation of the *veselija*, a cash donation to help pay for the party and maybe give the newlyweds a "nest egg."

Crisis. But many younger men, although they have enjoyed food, liquor, entertainment, sneak off without paying. The family is plunged into despair: the party costs hundreds of dollars (a year's wages for one stockyards worker). Chapter 1 ends with mixed feelings. Jurgis, sobered by this unexpected financial setback, carries frightened Ona to their house, reassuring her: "Leave it to me.... I will earn more ... I will work harder."

Ebb-and-flow of moods. Chapter 1 has moved from exuberant excitement to exhaustion, from gaiety to anxiety with grim hope.

CHARACTERIZATION

Through detailed accounts of how people look and act, Sinclair creates several distinctive characters "in the round." He depicts Jurgis through *contrasts*: he is big, powerful, strong-faced with black hair, black eyes, beetle-brows, yet in the social affair he looks shy and "frightened as a hunted animal"; but at the end, he is protective of his sixteen-year-old bride. Ona is the extreme opposite, small even for her age, blue-eyed, fair, emotionally dependent. Marija is vigorous, short, broad-shouldered, strong-voiced, a hungry soul with something like a horse face. Tamoszius Kuszleika, leader of the three-piece orchestra, five feet tall, with a "wizened up," comical face, plays out of tune but passionately.

Three older characters *foreshadow* the future that might await the younger workers. Antanas, once healthy in the Lithuanian outdoors, is now consumptive. Jokubas, though fat and healthy, has mortgaged his store in the face of economic hardship. Widow Aniele supports her children partly by laboring long hours as a washerwoman; the children scavenge for garbage to feed their chickens.

THEMES AND NATURALISM

Sinclair thus launches his book on *Zolaist, naturalistic premises*. He sees his duty as novelist first of all to indicate how heredity, environment, and cultural background shape character and determine people's fate. He represents lower-class people as trapped by economic circumstances, victims of an exploitive profit system. They work long days for low pay and must send even their children out to work; if they are one minute late, they are docked a whole hour's pay; if they are hurt in their dangerous meat-cutting, they are not compensated for lost time or for medical expenses; the saloonkeeper serves them two half-kegs of beer and charges them for two full kegs. Their economic masters engage freely in such greedy practices because the politicians are on the side of the businessmen.

As a Zolaist, Sinclair is especially interested in the *effects of a change in environment*. This is what the *acziavimas-veselija* situation signifies. In Lithuania, every reveler would solemnly — communally — have paid his share of the newlyweds' expenses; but in America, the younger men seemingly have learned that selfish irresponsibility pays off; rugged individualism is "smart." Sinclair adapts a Zolaist principle: "a rule made in the forests of Lithuania is hard to apply in the stockyards district of Chicago." And his characters were healthier in the "green meadows and . . . snowclad hills" of Europe than in "Chicago and its slums."

OTHER TECHNIQUES

Naturalistic documentation. A Zolaist does a thorough reporting job, documenting exact details of time, place, custom. Hence Sinclair identifies the "two step" as "the fashion" in dancing and "In the Good Old Summertime" as a current hit song; he notes how men wax their mustaches and oil a curl to plaster it to the forehead.

Sense appeal. Sinclair achieves authenticity largely through his appeal to our senses. We *hear* the "broom, broom" sound of a cello and the "squeaking" of fiddles; *smell* the "heavy scent" of drinkers "reeking" with alcohol; *see* designs on vest and shirt, and the changing pattern of the dance: "what had once been the ring had now the shape of a pear, with Marija at the stem . . . ."

Symbolism and simile. Sinclair relies heavily on *similes,* figures of speech that interest us because they establish similarities between dissimilar things. Thus Jurgis looks like "a hunted animal," a violinist like "an overdriven mule," Elzbieta is "in a flutter like a hummingbird," Tamoszius "throbs like a runaway steam engine." Certain actions are *symbolic:* they stand for something larger than themselves. Thus the Chicago *veselija* represents changing social attitudes caused by a change of environment. And no matter what excitement is created by violinists playing in the treble, the bass player still saws his "lugubrious" notes. This symbolically *foreshadows* the dual mood of the party: joy of the revelers underscored by gloom of the family.

Literary allusion. Sinclair at one point describes Marija's feelings thus: "Her soul cried out in the words of Faust, 'Stay, thou art fair!' " The allusion is to the drama *Faust* by J.W. von Goethe (1749 – 1832). Doctor Faust agrees that if ever he finds any moment so fair he wants it to last — if ever he acts satisfied — the devil may take his soul.

Foreign phrases. Sinclair does not translate many of the Lithuanian phrases that his characters use. Instead, he makes their meaning clear in context. He employs them mainly for the Old World ambience they provide.

Experimentation with tenses. Sinclair recounts the wedding party mainly in the past tense but in two long passages he shifts to the present tense. Thus he "zooms in" for greater immediacy, and he accustoms us to a flexible time perspective.

Chapter 2

PLOT DEVELOPMENT

In Chapter 1, Sinclair aroused our interest with a colorful social event. Now he begins a *series of flashbacks* to satisfy our curiosity about his characters' past history. To explain it in more technical terms: In Chapter 1, he launched his story *in medias res* (Latin: in the middle of things); now he provides *exposition*, or background information.

Change of environment. In Lithuania these people had been oppressed by their socioeconomic superiors. Jurgis had suffered cruel treatment as a railroad worker, Ona's family had been cheated by a bribe-taking judge, Marija was a servant beaten by her master. They thought of America as a land where everyone would be equal and "might do as he pleased," where indeed, a Lithuanian named Szedvilas had made a fortune in Chicago. Six adults plus Elzbieta's six children, they set out for America, lost much of their savings to scheming uniformed officials in New York, and wound up bewildered in filthy, smoky, smelly Chicago. Szedvilas, it developed, was only running a delicatessen; he sent them to live with the washerwoman Aniele, who packed six people to a room in her boarding house. The reader might infer that these immigrants had simply swapped one bad situation for another, that the plight of the lower classes was the same in both Old and New Worlds. But Jurgis was impressed with the technological ingenuity evident in America. Chapter 2 ends with his confidence he could make it in the land "of opportunity and freedom."

CHARACTERIZATION

Sinclair lets us see the newcomer Jurgis through the eyes of veteran Chicago workers. They tried to tell him how men were "broken" by the heavy work in the stockyards. But he "was like . . . a boy from the country," confident that his youth and strength would triumph and that only weaklings could be "beaten" by hard work. Thus Sinclair uses the literary device of the *naif* — a naive character who starts out innocent, trusting the system, and must learn the facts of life the hard way. In the process, presumably *the reader also learns how to distinguish illusion from reality.*

OTHER TECHNIQUES

Naturalistic elements. In Chapter 2, Sinclair continues to use a Zolaist approach. Before Jurgis fell in love with Ona, he had laughed at marriage "as a foolish trap for a man to walk into." This is a familiar naturalistic theme: that sex lures a person into economic difficulties and limits his freedom. Sinclair also follows Zola's lead in refusing to ignore the sordid aspects of life: *the naturalist believes that unless the whole truth is told, the novelist is using art to deceive.* Thus Sinclair describes the ugly dwellings, "filthy creek," "smoke, thick, oily, and black as night." He describes what no "polite" writer of the day would mention: vermin that infested the mattresses in Aniele's boarding house, children scraping in garbage for food. Pointedly, Sinclair says, "The place had an odor for which there are no polite words."

Sense appeal. Again, the chapter is rich in its appeal to the reader's senses. The stockyards gave off "an elemental odor, raw and crude . . . almost rancid" and "a sound made up of ten thousand little sounds": the distant lowing of cattle and grunting of swine. In the light of sunset, sordid smoke became "black and brown and gray and purple . . . a dream of wonder."

Figures of speech. Again, Sinclair uses poetic devices to enrich his description. A typical *simile* (a comparison expressed using the words *as* or *like*): "the tops of the houses shone like fire." Typical metaphors (comparisons made without equal signs): "the river of smoke," "the great sore of a city."

Chapter 3

PLOT DEVELOPMENT

Sinclair continues his exposition through flashbacks. Jurgis' confidence in his superiority over "weaklings" was borne out when he got a job in the yards on his first try. The "bosses noticed his form towering above the rest" on the line of applicants, many of whom had been applying for months without success. Not required to report for work until the next day, Jurguis celebrated by going with Jokubas and the others to see "the sights of Packingtown": two hundred fifty miles of track within the yards that brought in ten thousand cattle, ten thousand hogs, five thousand sheep every day, or eight to ten million "creatures turned into food every year"; within the plants, long lines of men working furiously as machinery passed the animals from worker to worker, each of whom performed a specialized task in slaughtering, cutting up, packing of meat. Nothing was wasted: animal fat was made into soap, feet into glue, bones into fertilizer.

Conflict of views. Jokubas whispered that as visitors, taken on a guided tour, they "did not see any more than the packers wanted them to" — for example, they did not see "the secret rooms where . . . spoiled meats went to be doctored." But Jurgis was annoyed with Jokubas' criticisms: the giant immigrant stood in awe of these feats of mechanical engineering that furnished food for thirty million people all over the world.

CHARACTERIZATION

Sinclair continues to portray Jurgis as the naif who persisted in believing in the fairness of the system in spite of what more experienced people told him. At the chapter's end, "the boy from the country" felt glad he was now part of this system which, he thought, would repay his hard labor by becoming "responsible for his welfare."

OTHER LITERARY TECHNIQUES

Naturalism. The guided tour, as a quick way of giving the reader an overview of a large enterprise, was a favorite device of the Zolaists. For example, in George Moore's *A Mummer's Wife* (1885), the first Zolaist novel in English, the main characters go on a tour of the pottery works of Hanley. Sinclair is also using a naturalistic method in his *detailed attention to work techniques* — for example, exactly how the "cleaver men" chopped a carcass, how the packing plants were designed to make the hogs walk to the top floor to be slaughtered so that gravity would move their carcasses to the various stations on the lower floors!

In his *naturalistic attention to the social climate*, Sinclair describes how even as early as 1904, John Q. Citizen considered advertising signs that "defaced the landscape" as one of "the torments of his life." America was proclaiming its materialism "on every street corner." And as a Socialist, Sinclair criticizes the antitrust laws that force corporations to "be deadly rivals . . . to try to ruin each other"; in other words, to engage in wasteful competition instead of socialized collaboration.

Allegory. After evoking our sympathy for the squeaking, agonizing, dying animals, largely through the horror of the women in the party, Sinclair draws an implicit parallel between animal life and human life. The hogs "were so very human in their protests." Each one "had gone about his business" while "a horrid Fate waited in his pathway." Ironically, Jurgis muttered, "I'm glad I'm not a hog." Such narration — in which the surface story hides a second meaning — is called *allegory*.

But perhaps Sinclair's allegory misfires. The passage is so drenched in sentimentality and triteness — "was one to believe . . . there was nowhere a god of hogs . . .?" — that it verges on absurd bathos rather than tragic feeling. On the intellectual level, however, Sinclair makes his point: Jurgis and all his kind were like dumb animals, "trusting and strong in faith," who were being herded toward eventual slaughter by the people in control.

Other comparisons. Sinclair continues to use numerous similes and metaphors to keep his narrative alive. The plant employees worked furiously like battling football players, and the cattle driven through the chutes formed "a very river of death."

Foreshadowing. Both Jokubas' negative remarks and the allegory of the hogs serve as foreshadowing of the fate of Jurgis, Ona, and the other new arrivals.

Chapter 4

PLOT DEVELOPMENT

Sinclair continues to tell his story with almost breathtaking speed. Chapter 4 is an especially good example of his racy narration; of his control of the ebb and flow of feelings, from optimism to despair and back; of his admiration for the heroism of everyday life, especially of innocent people facing a hostile world.

Flow. The flashbacks continue to unfold the characters' adventures before the wedding. Three of the adults had gotten jobs: Jurgis on the killing beds, wading in blood twelve hours a day, sweeping entrails into traps in the floor; Marija in a canning room, painting cans, skilled piecework that paid more than Jurgis' job; Jonas, Elzbieta's brother, pushing a hand truck. Only Dede Antanas remained unemployed. According to Szedvilas, it was "the rule everywhere in America" that employers "did not keep the men who had grown old in their . . . service — to say nothing of taking on new ones." Jurgis was determined that Ona and Elzbieta would stay at home to run the house. Although the twelve-year-old son of Szedvilas had already been working for a year, Jurgis wanted Elzbieta's six children to go to school.

Ebb. On this tide of good feeling, the immigrants became easy prey for a crooked real estate firm. Their advertising — "own your own home for less than your rent" — offered them a new two-story house for sale by mortgage. In actuality, the house they bought was an old (but newly painted) one-story house with unfloored attic and basement, and the contract actually described their eight years of payments as rent. After terrible agonies during the negotiations — Jokubas Szedvilas assured them they were being swindled — they learned from a lawyer that the "property was said to be merely rented until the last payment had been made . . . to make it easier to turn the party out if he did not make the payments." With his usual work-ethic confidence that he need only "work harder" to succeed, Jurgis was glad to pay the lawyer, although this arrangement earned him no equity at all in the house until he would make the final payment! Failure to make any payment could result in his losing months or years of his investment. The chapter ends with the women "sobbing softly" because of the emotional strain of the harrowing negotiations.

CHARACTERIZATION

Sinclair further develops Jurgis as a *naif*, and continues to use the more experienced Jokubas as a *foil*. (Foil is the technical name for a character that, by contrast, emphasizes the nature of another character. The term comes from the jewelry trade, in which a thin foil is placed under a gem to lend it brilliance.)

The chapter reveals other facets of Jurgis' makeup. He was a male supremacist, believing that his future wife should have no career outside the home (a position Sinclair satirizes by showing that Marija could command greater pay in the outside world than Jurgis could). And Jurgis was capable of violent wrath. When he stormed off to get a lawyer to explain the suspicious "deed," the women thought he "had gone to murder the agent." Sinclair smoothly portrays the agent as a type: the fast-talking salesman who could sell an electric refrigerator to an Eskimo living in an unwired igloo.

Meanwhile, the author has developed his contrast between the more worldly, competent, prepossessing Marija and the shy, protected Ona: one woman as a foil for another.

NATURALISTIC THEMES AND MUCKRAKING

Sinclair further documents his indictment of the politico-economic system, portraying the powerless as victimized by the powerful. The system had no more responsibility for its aging worker than it had for its injured worker; the law connived at twelve-year-olds working in industrial plants and at real estate men's engaging in shady practices.

Chapter 5

PLOT DEVELOPMENT AND NATURALISM

Continuing the flashbacks, Chapter 5 offers perhaps the simplest example of Sinclair's *ebb-and-flow structure*. In the first part of the chapter, all the characters were happy in their "nest feathering"; in the second part, all four wage earners in the house were beginning to be disillusioned with their situation.

Flow. Concern with naturalistic detail and techniques dominates the first part. We learn how an extended family of twelve working-class people crowded into a four-room house with only one bed; how the dining table went into the kitchen so the dining room could be used as bedroom for Elzbieta and her children; how Jurgis made chests of drawers out of packing cases; and how they used lard instead of butter. Their happiness in feathering their nest is accompanied by a rare burst of humor as Sinclair parodies the advertising that instructs them how they could "furnish all the necessary feathers" by signing "another paper" — by entering the trap of installment buying.

Ebb. In the second part, six rapid-fire revelations at the packing plants began to shatter "Jurgis' faith in things as they are": (1) Jurgis observed the "speed-up" system: the bosses paid higher wages to men manning positions that determined the pace at which all the other workers had to function. Working fiendishly, these "pacemakers" soon wore out and were replaced. Organizing opposition to the speed-up, a union delegate tried to enroll Jurgis. But Jurgis honestly had no idea that he had any rights except to "do as he was told." (2) Antanas was finally able to get a job only by "kicking back" a third of his wages to a boss; he was shocked to discover that he was expected to sweep refuse into the meat vats. (3) When Jurgis questioned Tamoszius, who folded hides, about the bribes Antanas had to pay, Jurgis was told that graft pervaded the system: "nobody rose in Packingtown by doing good work . . . if you met a man who was rising . . . you met a knave." The system would reward a labor spy but would punish an honest man by "speeding him up," wearing him down, throwing him out. (4) Marija learned how she had gotten a job so easily: a woman with fifteen years' service and a child to support was fired because of illness. (5) Jonas learned that he had been hired to replace a man crushed by the heavy hand truck because the "speed-up" created unsafe working conditions. (6) Finally Jurgis himself saw routine violations of the law: pregnant cows and their calves, as well as dead cattle, were butchered daily and added to the legal meat. This was accomplished by having a boss talk to an inspector while "slunk" calves were being processed, or by doing the work after hours when the inspectors had gone home. Jurgis was now able to see why some people had "laughed at him for his faith in America."

NATURALISTIC CHARACTERIZATION

Jurgis the naif was becoming a skeptic. *The characters were trapped by a competitive system that values profits more than people.* All the workers Jurgis met "hated their work . . . the bosses . . . the owners." Even the brightest part of the chapter, the parody of advertising slogans, represents Americans as brainwashed.

STYLE

For most of the chapter, Sinclair's tone is grimmer, more factual, unrelieved by dialogue, prosaic, lacking the frequent figures of speech that made the earlier chapters so poetic.

Chapter 6

PLOT DEVELOPMENT AND NATURALISM

Chapter 6 begins and ends on the same note: Jurgis and Ona were "very much in love." Yet most of this last full chapter of flashbacks is devoted to the reasons their wedding was delayed "into the second year" in America — devoted, that is, to detailing more of the naturalistic entrapment of their lives.

Change of environment. First of all, Antanas and Elzbieta had wanted the lovers to wait until they had enough friends and money to enjoy a traditional wedding feast with the advantages of the *veselija*. Sinclair's already having recounted the feast in Chapter 1 has made it possible for the reader to appreciate now the sad irony of the elders' hopes. There "was a fear in . . . these two, lest this journey to a new country somehow undermine the old home virtues of their children." Again the reader can appreciate the reality of this fear: *the naturalist theme of the consequences of changing environment is now well established.*

Naturalistic entrapment. Furthermore, from an elderly neighbor, Grandmother Majauskiene, Jurgis' household had learned more details about their deal with the real estate man. The builders deliberately sold these flimsy, overpriced houses "with the idea that . . . people who bought them would not be able to pay for them." Injuries on the job, failure to endure the "speed-up," illness from bad working and living conditions would ultimately force most "buyers" to skip a payment and then "lose the house and all . . . they had paid." They could easily be replaced by new immigrants: "old man Durham," the packing tycoon, had sent agents into Europe "to spread the tale of . . . high wages at the stockyards." Finally, Mrs. Majauskiene revealed to the newcomers what the real-estate man had failed to tell them about their payments (and what they, unlettered in English, could not read in the "deed"): they had contracted to pay not only a mortgage payment of twelve dollars a month, but also seven dollars a month interest. Result: Ona and Elzbieta's fourteen-year-old boy Stanislovas had to be sent out to work after all.

NATURALISTIC CHARACTERIZATION

A main Zolaist concept of human destiny is summed up in Sinclair's sentence: "As if in a flash of lightning, they saw themselves — victims of a relentless fate, trapped, in the grip of destruction." And the naturalistic conception of *sex as part of the entrapment* is reinforced by the old lady's boasting she had been able to pay for her house because her son "had had sense enough not to marry."

Indeed, Sinclair draws a striking picture of old Mrs. Majauskiene. She obviously enjoyed being the one to reveal all these horrors to a household of innocents. She became a fearsome symbol to her tortured listeners, "typifying fate" as she croaked "like some dismal raven." And she serves to foreshadow later plot developments: she was a Socialist, the first we meet.

Sinclair depicts Stanislovas as a brave little man, glad to help out, oblivious to the fact that he had now been consigned to the hopeless life of the unschooled, unskilled worker.

In characterizing Stanislovas, Sinclair puts *naturalistic emphasis on the techniques of survival*. We learn that the only way this fourteen-year-old could get a job was to get his priest to certify that he was sixteen. And we learn in detail the operation he had to perform: "how to place a lard can everytime the empty arm of the remorseless machine came to him." He performed this monotonous task ten hours a day, in an unheated cellar, as one of 1,750,000 child laborers in the United States.

Chapter 7

PLOT DEVELOPMENT

Structure. Sinclair develops his chapter in three parts: (1) a brief introduction completes the flashbacks and brings us up to the time of the wedding feast described in Chapter 1. (2) The middle section describes the horrible conditions under which the newlyweds began their marriage. (3) The last part develops according to a Darwinist analogy about the "survival of the fittest."

Jurgis and Ona start out in debt from the financial setback of the *veselija* (Chapter 1): "Over them . . . there cracked the lash of want." Embittered Jurgis now sees life as "a war of each against all . . . the devil take the hindmost." Typical of their plight: Ona suffers a serious cold because as a working girl, she "did not own waterproofs" and takes ill going to work in the rain. Antanas dies of consumption, and Jurgis, now wily, learns how to protect himself against businessmen who try to cheat him over funeral expenses.

Analogy. Sinclair develops their winter sufferings by a comparison of people to branches of a tree: "storms strew the ground with . . . weaker branches." Stanislovas develops a terror of going to work in freezing weather when a fellow child laborer loses his ears to frostbite. Jurgis and his mates on the killing beds work without heat. An "annual harvest" of winter illness kills many ill-clad, ill-housed workers, but through every blizzard, "starving and penniless men" are waiting to take the place of the dead and dying. In their thirty-minute lunch period, the men rush to saloons that offer "free lunch" to anyone buying a drink. The Rudkus household plod through each day a little nearer to the time when they too will be "shaken from the tree."

CHARACTERIZATION

Again Sinclair uses the naturalist emphasis on environmental influence. The children "were not as well as they had been at home": their cabins in Lithuania were better than their Chicago house. Here they live over a cesspool containing fifteen years' drainage, drink the watered-down milk and eat the adulterated food sold in lower-class neighborhoods. Sinclair also sees the "free-lunch" trick as conditioning the worker to seek solace in liquor.

Significantly, the two characters who should not be working at all — sickly old Antanas and fourteen-year-old Stanislovas — are the ones who break down first — one physically, the other mentally.

Jurgis and Ona continue to develop as extreme contrasts. Jurgis is the protector who feels guilty he cannot give Ona a better life; even while out working, she seems dependent and passive.

OTHER LITERARY DEVICES

Naturalistic documentation. Sinclair not only describes a sordid life that most writers and their publishers would prefer to ignore, but he also observes sarcastically, "How . . . could any one . . . excite sympathy among lovers of good literature by telling how a family found their home alive with vermin . . .?" Finding roach powder expensive yet ineffective, Jurgis resigns himself to sharing his quarters with bugs.

Foreshadowing. Sinclair foreshadows future tragedies when, at the start, Jurgis drinks enough to get the free lunch, and Ona wonders why her forewoman seems to want her girls not to marry. Neither knows what these circumstances can lead to.

Style. Sinclair remains at his best in writing with vigorous indignation over social conditions or when using an analogy to structure his action. He is at his worst in representing deep emotion: his second paragraph, describing Jurgis and Ona's "trampled" love, verges again on trite sentimentality.

Literary allusion. To explain how Antanas "fell to pieces, all at once and in a heap," Sinclair likens him to the One-Horse Shay. This is the subject of Oliver Wendell Holmes' poem, "The Deacon's Masterpiece or The Wonderful One-Horse-Shay," to be found in his book *Autocrat of the Breakfast Table.*

Chapter 8

PLOT DEVELOPMENT

Structure. Again, Sinclair develops a chapter by ebb and flow, this time a rise and fall in the life of Marija followed by a fall in the hopes of Jurgis.

Motif repeated. Sinclair repeats his *motif of love stymied by economics* as he develops a romance between Marija and Tamoszius that in some respects runs *parallel* to the Ona – Jurgis romance. Since the wedding feast (Chapter 1), the little musician has loved the powerful woman, whose admiration for his talent blossoms into sexual passion. The Rudkus family benefits from his music and the fact that Marija returns from his party performances laden with food. Then Marija's plant closes during a slump, the Rudkus household loses its biggest salary, and the new lovers must postpone their wedding date.

Crisis or turning point. Men on the killing beds also suffer from the slump. They average now not eleven but six hours a day, with no pay for "broken time": arriving a minute late, a man is docked for the whole hour; he is not paid for any fraction of an hour required to complete the day's work! The second time the union organizer approaches him, Jurgis — and all the workers in his family — become unionists: "he understood that a fight was on . . . it was his fight."

CHARACTERIZATION

Three characters develop significantly in this chapter. Jurgis casts his lot no longer with the Establishment but with organized labor. The new lovers overcome a barrier: social prejudice against a relationship between a frail man and a powerful woman. Tamoszius learns that for all her "violence," Marija has a gentle soul, while she realizes that in his music, he is also powerful. Sinclair develops his affectionate contrast of these two by depicting Marija as an outspoken unionist, and Tamoszius as shy with words.

NATURALISTIC DOCUMENTATION

Sinclair continues, in Zolaist fashion, to tell the full truth about areas of life not usually mentioned in "polite" literature. Thus we suffer with Jurgis as he is forced into close contact with a man with bad breath. We understand why, when Marija and Tamoszius "sit for hours in the kitchen," the others pretend not to know what's going on.

Chapter 9

PLOT DEVELOPMENT AND MUCKRAKING

Structure. The action is minimal. Sinclair exploits the fact that Jurgis, as a union member, has learned to talk politics. Thus Sinclair can recite the social and political evils that Jurgis sees or hears about. Again Sinclair uses a flashback, this time only two paragraphs long, to tell us that when Jurgis was still a *naif*, his naturalization as a citizen had been arranged by his bosses —

industrial and political — so that he could be duped into voting their way, with a bonus of two dollars, on Election Day.

Naturalistic documentation. Chapter 9 constitutes *a catalogue of political and industrial abuses such as muckrakers were exposing at the time.* Chicago is run by a political boss, Scully, who stays in power through political patronage, bribes to voters like Jurgis, and use of public resources for private gain. American democratic government is described as rule by parties that are "two rival sets of grafters." Jurgis finds that "here, precisely as in Russia . . . rich men owned everything."

Evils in the packing industry, Sinclair's own special domain, include pollution of the Chicago River by packing plants; sale of contaminated meat; selling horse meat as beef, goat meat as lamb, various meat wastes as "potted chicken" or "deviled ham." Sinclair also reminds his readers of the "embalmed beef" that "had killed several times as many United States soldiers as all the bullets of the Spaniards" in the Spanish-American War.

Sinclair is so intent on thoroughly documenting his disclosures of the "spoiled meat industry" that he uses an all-out journalistic technique in a novel: to support his sarcastic point that "inspectors . . . were paid by the United States . . . to certify that all the diseased meat was kept in the state," he uses a four-paragraph footnote quoting from U.S. "Rules and Regulations."

He ends his chapter listing occupational diseases and injuries that Packingtown workers incur in the line of duty — like sores from acids, blood poisoning from cuts, hands lost in the machinery — concluding with his famous controversial example of men who fell into the vats and "had gone out into the world as Durham's Pure Leaf Lard."

CHARACTERIZATION

Sinclair contrasts Jurgis with Jonas. Jurgis struggles toward understanding. Jonas is really becoming corrupt and cynical. He volunteers to vote three times in one day, for a price. The author also gives us striking sketches of two new characters: A sinister, unnamed "night watchman" acts as go-between in Jurgis' and Jonas' naturalization and polling-booth adventures; Scully is portrayed as a thoroughly corrupt political boss, a type in the day's news.

OTHER TECHNIQUES

Poetic description. The poet in Sinclair reappears in his metaphoric descriptions of the polluted "Bubbly Creek," which is constantly in motion, "as if huge fish were feeding in it"; in places, "the grease and filth have caked solid, and the creek looks like a bed of lava."

Literary allusions. Hearing a certain butcher who processed carcasses for canning, says Sinclair, "would have been worth while for a Dante or a Zola." Dante (1265 – 1321) was author of *The Inferno*, a poetic treatment of the evils of *his* day. Zola (1840 – 1902) was the father of the naturalistic novel and the great muckraker of France.

Chapter 10

PLOT DEVELOPMENT AND NATURALISM

Nature and structure of plot. Chapter 10 is another section that reads more like a social worker's case history than a section of a novel. There are no real scenes, no dialogue. Summaries of action and conditions predominate. The story follows Sinclair's by now familiar ebb-and-flow structure.

Ebb. In despair, Marija gives up all idea of marrying at this time. Jurgis discovers other charges in his "deed" not covered in the real estate advertising or in the verbal negotiations: insurance, taxes, sewer and sidewalk levies. He realizes that in America "people who worked with their hands were a class apart, and . . . made to feel it." When the canning plant reopens, Marija is recalled but her union activities cause her to be fired. She steps down from "skilled worker" as can painter to manual laborer in a packing plant. Ona discovers her forewoman "lived in a bawdy house" and the reader, if not *naif* Ona, can see this as the reason the forelady dislikes married women: they are not so easy to recruit as prostitutes.

Flow. Ona gives birth to a big boy, whose arrival makes Jurgis proudly brace himself anew "for the struggle, for the sake of that tiny mote of human possibility."

Ebb. But Ona cannot breastfeed (working-class women return to work soon after childbirth or starve) and so the child is fed "the pale blue poison that was called milk" in working-class stores and Ona develops "womb trouble" from the lack of rest after childbirth.

NATURALISTIC ELEMENTS

Themes. The dominant theme of the chapter (but unstated) is Engel's Law — "the curse of the poor is their poverty." Indebtedness keeps them off-balance in the struggle for existence. A familiar naturalistic theme — well borne out by historians of the Victorian Age — is that technological society drives women into prostitution. Another influence of technology on social conditions is evident in the fact that Jurgis, as a factory worker, has less chance to be with his offspring than agricultural workers have to be with theirs.

Naturalistic detail. Sinclair again goes into social and physiological details that in his day were not discussed in "polite" literature: how workers on the killing beds developed a foul body odor; how girls drift into bawdy houses as a matter of survival; how "womb troubles" cause pains and depression that drive women to crave liquor as a painkiller. Sinclair's knowledge of "womb troubles," as we have seen, was based on his wife Meta's postpartum difficulties.

Naturalistic characterization. Jurgis' character develops mainly in reactions to his environment. His demands that the agent explain all expenses incurred by his signing the "deed" are delivered "with sarcasm proper to the new way of life he had learned." And the biological miracle of seeing a tiny replica of himself makes Jurgis a man of deeper emotions and even of philosophical reflection.

Naturalistic simile. In the bare case-history style Sinclair uses in Chapter 10, poetic devices are rare. The best is a bitter figure of speech that only a Zolaist would think of: "midwives . . . grow as thick as fleas in Packingtown" because workers cannot afford physicians.

Chapter 11

PLOT DEVELOPMENT AND NATURALISM

Nature and structure of plot. Sinclair continues to relate not so much a fictionalized account as a kind of typical case history of a disadvantaged family. Things now go mainly downhill for the Rudkus household, resulting in a *chronicle of disasters*, with only the most ironic of consolations.

Naturalistic emphasis on accident. As a Zolaist, Sinclair stresses how *accidents determine fate*, how *any chance event can be a greater calamity to the poor than to the rich*. Two accidents figure here. When police try to arrest a drunkard in front of a bank, a crowd gathers, workers passing by mistakenly assume there is "a run on the bank," and an endless line forms to draw out their savings! (In those days, bank accounts were not insured by the government: when a bank failed, depositors lost their savings.) Then a steer runs amok on the killing beds, and in his flight Jurgis turns an ankle. "The injury was not one that Durham and Company could be held responsible for!" So Jurgis is sent home to bed; Ona pays the bills out of their meager savings. Even Jurgis' one consolation in his unemployment is accidental: only when bedridden can he enjoy the company of his son Antanas.

Change of environment. Continually Sinclair stresses the effect on his characters of their change of diet. For example, in Lithuania they ate real sausage; here they eat imitation sausage, made of potato flour which "has no more food value than so much wood" and is therefore illegal — in Europe, anyway.

CHARACTERIZATION

Jurgis finally realizes that even a powerful man, willing to work hard, can be beaten by the system and circumstances. His philosophical growth is indicated by his awareness now that selling his vote is unethical, but he remains a hopeless male supremacist, convinced that simply by being a man he is smarter than Marija. Even Sinclair himself seems guilty of male chauvinism as he says that Elzbieta's efforts to console Jurgis are part of the "age-long and everlasting hypocrisy of woman." In tending to find a biological basis in behavior, naturalists often risk hypotheses like this one.

Style, similes, allusion. The style is as bleak as the subject matter, except that Sinclair finds some poignant hope in the father-son relationship: "Look . . . he knows his papa . . . the little rascal!" Similes are there but are rather trite: "Jurgis would get cross as any bear." The thought of being defeated " was like an icy hand at his heart." In battling a blizzard that knocks out weaker men, he feels like "some monarch of the forest that has vanquished his foes . . . and then falls into some . . . trap."

Again Sinclair uses a literary allusion more out of his own than out of his characters' experience. "It was for all the world the story of Prometheus bound." In Greek mythology, and in a play by Aeschylus, Prometheus steals fire from heaven to improve man's condition. He is punished for 30,000 years by Zeus who has him chained to a rock and sends a bird to peck at his liver.

Chapter 12

PLOT DEVELOPMENT AND NATURALISM

Chapter 12 comprises yet another chronicle of disasters unrelieved by even a line of dialogue or a ray of cheer. Jurgis loses his job; Stanislovas' hand is disabled by frostbite; Jonas disappears — slipping into a vat or quitting such a dismal household for a better scene? — two more children, Vilimas, age eleven, and Nikalojus, ten, must quit school and go to work, and Jurgis joins the army of the unemployed.

Sinclair again emphasizes techniques of survival. We learn how little boys become newspaper dealers against adult competition and deception, how they learn to cheat on carfare, how the packing-company lawyers cheat injured workers out of their rights.

CHARACTERIZATION

A major Zolaist theme is that industrialized society brutalizes the worker. Jurgis becomes dull, Ona fears he is no longer capable of love, he beats Stanislovas to drive him out to work, and he is no longer a prepossessing physical specimen but a seedy-looking wretch.

OTHER LITERARY DEVICES

Literary allusions. Sinclair incorporates a famous phrase from Francis Bacon's *Essays* (1625) into his naturalistic description of "Poor Tamoszius," who "had fallen in love and so *given hostages to fortune,* and was doomed to be dragged down too." (italics Bacon's)

Metaphors. Sinclair ends his indignant description of working-class horrors with a burst of metaphors. Jurgis had been used by the packers and "now he was . . . a damaged article," joining those beaten people "ground up in other mills," "worn-out parts of the great merciless packing machine."

Chapter 13

PLOT DEVELOPMENT

Structure. After two chapters of recounting unrelieved calamities, Sinclair returns to a pattern of the ebb and flow of fortune. But again, he uses a steady narration unrelieved by dialogue. The literary effect is a partial dehumanization of events.

Ebb. Elzbieta's youngest child, three-year-old crippled Kristoforas (the name means "bearer of a cross") eats sausage made from adulterated pork and dies of convulsions. Jurgis is so desperate for money he takes a job in the most hazardous occupation of all: making fertilizer. "Breathing their lungs full of fine dust," fertilizer workers are "doomed to die" in a short order.

Flow. But at least Jurgis can pay his debts and get the "lowest man's" share of a "summer of prosperity" in America. And now that little Kotrina is old enough to do the housework, Elzbieta is able to go out and get a job. Thus Vilimas and Nikalojus can return to school.

NATURALISTIC ELEMENTS

Effects of environment. The little newsboys had been "taking on the tone of their environment," learning to smoke and gamble; they were already familiar with saloons and bawdyhouses and with sleeping in empty hallways or under trucks.

Emphasis on survival techniques. Sinclair describes in detail how fertilizer is made, how Jurgis has to tie a sponge over his mouth as he shovels fertilizer into trucks, and how Elzbieta, "a servant of a 'sausage machine,'" "worked so fast that the eye could not follow her," "twisting sausage links and racing with death." The chapter ends with a reference to "ruthless economic laws" that drive a poor woman to work this way while "well dressed ladies and gentlemen," on a guided tour of her plant, "stare at her, as at some wild beast in a menagerie." Again, *naturalism sees technology as brutalizing human beings.*

Naturalistic detail. Zolaist Sinclair again describes what "polite society" prefers to ignore. Jurgis' work with fertilizer makes him smell so bad he never has any trouble getting a seat in a streetcar. He comes home caked with bone dust and rock dust and stinks up the house.

CHARACTERIZATION

Casualties are mounting in the war for survival: Dede Antanas and Kristoforas are dead, Jonas missing, Stanislovas injured physically, and Vilimas and Nikalojus psychologically.

But Jurgis and Elzbieta grow more self-sacrificing, nobler, in adversity. Jurgis overcomes his fear of the fertilizer plant and of the social ostracism it brings him, rather than see his family suffer further privation. Elzbieta, until now a housewife, spends her day as a virtual automaton in order to get her boys off the streets and into the classroom.

Chapter 14

PLOT DEVELOPMENT

Structure. Sinclair divides Chapter 14 into two parts, dealing first with further evils in the packing industry, then with worsening problems in the Rudkus household.

"Spoiled meat industry." Now that Elzbieta works in a sausage factory, and Marija in a cannery, the family has had many sources of inside information about "the Packingtown swindles." Jonas had told them about "the miracles of chemistry" performed in the pickling rooms to doctor up spoiled meat. Now Elzbieta knows how spoiled hams go into sausage; how rats, attracted to the meat and killed by rat poison, are swept — poison, rat dung, and all — together with the meat into the meat hoppers.

Domestic problems. With six more years of financial strain to pay off the mortgage, the Rudkus household members each fall into a private gloom. Elzbieta comes home stupefied from the exhausting, monotonous machine tending. Ona is often hysterical, for reasons foreshadowed (see Chapter 10) and thus inferable by the reader but still unknown to the others, who blame her condition on her being pregnant again. Jurgis has taken to drink to relieve his pain from his occupational and domestic life. The stage seems set for catastrophe.

NATURALISTIC ELEMENTS

Documentation of processes. In proper Zolaist fashion, Sinclair describes first the tools (white-hot iron, hollow needle attached to a pump) and chemicals (soda, borax, glycerine) used by packers to give spoiled meat "any color and any flavor and any odor" they choose, and later the methods used by Kotrina to handle Antanas' most recent infant illness: measles.

First-hand observation. Two situations are based on Sinclair's own life experience. As a boy he had observed his father's hopeless struggle with alcohol, here reflected in Jurgis' guiltily taking solace in drink. And as a recent father, Sinclair had observed how the illnesses of children were treated.

Naturalistic characterization. Persons driven to drink or to prostitution by pressures of circumstances are stock characters in naturalistic fiction. (See, for example, Zola's *The Dram Shop* and *Nana*, Moore's *A Mummer's Wife*, Stephen Crane's *Maggie: A Girl of the Streets*.) Jurgis' machismo figures in his taking to drink: "he would be a man again, and master of his life." The humiliation of his being a stinking fertilizer shoveler vanishes when he gets drunk, his "dead self" stirs in him, he finds himself "cracking jokes." In his guilt over thus raiding the family budget for liquor, he thinks the novel's fullest statement yet of the naturalistic view of sex as an economic trap: "It was all because he was a married man that he was compelled to stay in the yards; if it had not been for that he might have gone off like Jonas, and to hell with the packers. There were few single men in the fertilizer mill . . . ." Thus he falls into the psychological trap of blaming his woes not so much on the packers as on wife and son.

In explaining Elzbieta's state, Sinclair voices a common complaint against industrial work: "every faculty" that she did not need to take care of the machine was "crushed out of existence." Specialized work, sustained over long days, shrinks the personality.

STYLE AND METAPHOR

Again, Sinclair uses straight narration without dialogue. There is a rare burst of lyricism when "The gates of memory . . . roll open" and they think of happier times, but the general tone is evident from this metaphor: "their hopes were buried in separate graves."

Chapter 15

PLOT DEVELOPMENT

Structure and nature of plot. After several chapters in which he rarely used dialogue, preferring straight narration to dramatization, Sinclair now resumes the use of well-developed scenes that include extended conversation.

Introductory summary. Jurgis, Marija, Ona, Elzbieta are all working fifteen or sixteen hours a day during a rush season: to refuse to
work overtime is to be fired. Foreshadowing: Jurgis senses something in Ona's life "he was not allowed to know."

Extended scene. One night just before Thanksgiving, Ona does not
come home at all. Next morning, she says she stayed with Jadvyga
because "the cars had stopped running."

Transitional summary. The heavy cold lasts for a month, and morning after morning Jurgis half-carries Ona to work.

Extended scene. A few nights before Christmas, Ona again fails to
come home. In the morning Jurgis goes to Jadvyga's, where he
learns Ona has never stayed there. He discovers Elzbieta is also
lying to him. When he confronts Ona, demanding to know the truth,
she begs him to believe in her: it will be better for all concerned if he
takes things on faith. But in his fury he gets the truth out of her. Her
boss, Connor, has forced her to become his mistress (at Miss Henderson's "house downtown") by threatening to have them all — Ona,
Jurgis, Marija, Elzbieta — fired if she did not submit. Jurgis rushes
off to her place of work, beats up Connor, and is arrested.

NATURALISTIC ELEMENTS

Characterization. Bosses' use of economic power to force
women into sexual slavery is a typical naturalistic theme. Ona is
probably correct in pointing out that Connor "would have ruined
us," and "I only did it — to save us. It was our only chance." Jurgis cannot yet see that she was forced into prostitution the way
he was forced into hazardous fertilizer work: by unrelenting economic pressure. She is probably correct also in saying that the
affair would have soon been over: Connor "was getting tired of
me."

Brutalization. In Chapter 15 Sinclair stresses brutalization of
character that occurs in industrial society, as naturalism sees it.
Even before his discovery, Jurgis "lived like a dumb beast of
burden." On the streetcar on his way to beat up Connor, he looks
"like a wounded bull," and the passengers are not surprised: "a
man who smelled as Jurgis smelled should exhibit an aspect to
correspond." He closes with Connor as one would grapple with a
"great beast," and like a wild carnivore, he bites flesh out of Con-

nor's cheek. Of course, Ona has been the most brutalized of all. Her recurrent attacks of hysteria are now explained.

Naturalistic role of coincidence. Ona would have been "home late" instead of out all night, except that the cars had stopped running. "It was such a little thing — to ruin us all."

Naturalistic motif. For the fourth time, Sinclair states his motif of marriage delayed or prevented by economic hardship. Mikolas, the powerful beef boner we met in Chapter 1, has lost a hand on his job, and his marriage to Jadvyga "has been put off forever."

Truth and symbolism. Sinclair's fidelity to Zolaism *records facts of life that nonnaturalist writers avoid:* Jurgis' sacrilegious curses, the fact that he surprises Jadvyga when she's not quite dressed, that he smells of his occupation, that female employees may be sexually harassed by employers. Sinclair's timing of Ona's two nights away is symbolic in an ironic way: her sacrifices for her family are made just before Thanksgiving, just before Christmas.

Meaning of title. Sinclair's title now becomes fully justified. His characters truly live in the jungle: they are prey to beasts; they are themselves bestialized.

Chapter 16

PLOT DEVELOPMENT

Structure and nature. Sinclair divides Chapter 16 into three parts, consisting of Jurgis' *introspection* in jail, the *action* of his first trip to court, and his return to *introspection.*

Introspection. Jurgis now blames himself for allowing "Ona to work where she had . . . he had not stood between her and a fate . . . every one knew to be so common." He sees his act of violence as losing all of them their jobs and house, imagines their inevitable sufferings.

Action. Brought before a magistrate, Jurgis cannot put up three hundred dollars bail and is remanded to jail until the badly injured Connor can appear in court.

Introspection. To the sound of Christmas bells, Jurgis does his first serious thinking. He sees justice as a lie: *Connor is the wrongdoer but the law will be on his side.* The packers "had bought . . . the law." They had "murdered his father," "wrecked his wife," "cowed his family." *This is the first major crisis of the novel, the beginning of Jurgis' rebellion: society is now his enemy.*

CHARACTERIZATION, MUCKRAKING, AND METAPHOR

In naturalistic literature, it is fairly common for a main character to go down to total defeat (for example, Hurstwood in Dreiser's *Sister Carrie*, Kate in Moore's *A Mummer's Wife*). Jurgis has been wrong before in his resolve to succeed. Will he fail too in his outlawry?

Sinclair gives us another thumbnail sketch of a corrupt politician, Justice "Growler Pat" Callahan, who started his political life drawing two full-time salaries on the public payroll; he now owns brothels. Sinclair's metaphor: "If Scully was the thumb, Pat Callahan was the first finger of the unseen hand whereby the packers held down the people of the district."

NATURALISTIC TRUTH

In his Zolaist zeal to tell the whole truth, no matter how unpleasant, Sinclair notes that Jurgis' bedding in jail is full of fleas, bedbugs, lice, roaches; not even a thorough prison shower can remove the odor of fertilizer from his naked body; other outcasts in the jail make the air "fetid with their breath"; Ona's fate is "common."

LITERARY ALLUSION

Again Sinclair uses a literary allusion more out of his own world than out of his characters' lives. He ends Chapter 16 by quoting, in this order, lines 559 – 564, 535 – 538, and 555 – 558 of Oscar Wilde's "The Ballad of Reading Gaol" (1898), which dramatizes the cruelties of the penal system. "So wrote a poet, to whom the world has dealt its justice," says Sinclair, referring to the harsh imprisonment of Wilde — one of England's leading dramatists — for his sexual persuasion.

Chapter 17

PLOT DEVELOPMENT

Structure. Sinclair structures Chapter 17 in a sequence of *jail-court-jail* (like Chapter 16), but this time all three sections contain fully dramatized action on the *scene-summary-scene-summary* pattern (like Chapter 15).

Jail. Jurgis' new cellmate is a young safecracker who declared war on society after a "great company" had stolen his invention.

Trial. Judge Callahan accepts Connor's verision of the fight — Jurgis had attacked him because he had fired Ona — and sentences Jurgis to thirty days' hard labor.

Jail. Ironically, Stanislovas comes to the jail asking if Jurgis can help the family. Marija has cut her hand on the job; all the women are now unemployed; all the children, even Kotrina, are on the streets selling papers. The real estate agent is ready to foreclose.

NATURALISTIC ELEMENTS

Characterization and theme. Safecracker Jack Duane is a breezy fellow from another world: a college man, sophisticated, dapper. Through him, Sinclair reinforces the naturalistic theme that circumstances can force a man into a life of crime, especially if he becomes disillusioned with society and its justice. Poor Stanislovas is "growing" into a frightened defeatist.

Naturalistic truth and brutalization. Sinclair chronicles unpleasant truths that genteel middle-class literature ignores: when Jurgis moves in the upper bunk, roaches fall onto the lower; other prisoners call him "The Stinker" because of his fertilizer smell; imprisonment had completed the brutalization process for many prisoners, for whom "love was a beastliness, joy was a snare, and God was an imprecation," a curse. The phrase "joy was a snare" is a variation on Sinclair's motif that under an unstable economic system, flow must be followed by ebb.

Chapter 18

PLOT DEVELOPMENT

Structure. Again Sinclair develops a chapter by alternating *summary-scene-summary-scene.*

Introductory summary. Sinclair tells of Jurgis' last days in jail and his release.

Scene. Jurgis returns to "his" house, but it has been repainted; the roof and windows have been repaired. Irony: Out of Jurgis' house comes a "rosy-cheeked youngster, such as had never been seen in [Jurgis'] home before." In response to Jurgis' inquiries about his own family, the boy's mother says, "This is a new house. They told us so." Grandmother Majauskiene tells Jurgis where his family has gone.

Introspective summary. The dispossession of his family plunges Jurgis into a long review of his struggle in America, with stress on: "That trap of the extra payments that they . . . would never have attempted to pay! . . . the tricks of the packers . . . shutdowns . . . irregular hours . . . speeding-up . . . lowering of wages . . . raising of prices!"

Scene. Jurgis goes back to Aniele's boarding house to find Marija with a bandaged arm and Ona in premature labor crying out for the relief of death. There is no money for either doctor or midwife, but Aniele takes up a collection among the boarders, yielding Jurgis $1.25 with which to seek help.

NATURALISM AND MUCKRAKING

Being "free" again does not do Jurgis much good because — as Zolaism and Engel's law emphasize — the curse of the poor is their poverty. In every new situation, they are off-balance because of previous reverses. In addition to the attacks on the system quoted above, Sinclair salts other typical muckrakers' charges into the rapid action: open railroad crossings are "a deathtrap for the unwary"; the rain and the snow are filthy from pollution; and both the swindle of the resale of old houses as "new" and the cheating of a man out of his equity from his mortgage payments are confirmed.

Chapter 19

PLOT DEVELOPMENT

Chapter 19 unfolds in continuous action that rivals Chapter 1 for its richness of drama, scene, and characterization.

Jurgis finds a midwife, Madame Haupt, who demands twenty-five dollars for a birth but after much resistance agrees to accept Jurgis' pittance as a down payment. When the fat woman is finally at work up in Aniele's attic, Marija and Aniele send Jurgis away; traditionally, this is a female scene. A saloonkeeper, who remembers Jurgis as "a steady man" who "might be a good customer again," gives him drink, food, a place to rest. In the morning, Jurgis returns to a scene of disaster at Aniele's: the child stillborn, Ona recognizing Jurgis for just a moment before she dies. Ironically, Kotrina and the other newsvendors return with three dollars, which Jurgis cruelly appropriates: "I want to get drunk."

CHARACTERIZATION AND SIMILE

Ona, the most victimized of the twelve immigrants who had hoped for so much in America, is dead at eighteen. Jurgis has hit bottom, deprived of everything he came to America for — wife, house, job — and driven again to drink with the specter of outlawry hovering over him.

As usual, Sinclair excels in depicting new characters who figure briefly in the action. Madame Haupt is represented as a gross woman, living in filth, eating cheap food, but someone whose sense of responsibility can be invoked. Sinclair accords her one of his best similes: "when she walked she rolled like a small boat on the ocean." The saloonkeeper too is a compassionate man, a quiet observer of people. Sinclair can get beneath the externals — body, dress, housing — and find the real soul inside.

ENVIRONMENT

Chapter 19 offers some of the best descriptions of slum life to be found in *The Jungle*. Here we see a midwife living in squalor over a saloon, so unable to afford dental care her teeth are black; her patient lying in old rags in a garret of a crowded rooming house; a saloon keeper accustomed to letting a man "down on his luck" spend the night on the cellar stairs.

Chapter 20

PLOT DEVELOPMENT

Using both scenes and narration, Sinclair returns in Chapter 20 to his ebb-and-flow structure. Jurgis is convinced he must carry on for Antanas' sake. After Ona is buried in potter's field he tries to get work, but discovers he is blacklisted by the packing industry. He seems doomed to running errands for tips when a chance meeting with an old friend gets him a job in the harvester works. He thinks again of night school, advancement, security. Then one day his department is "closed until further notice."

NATURALISTIC ELEMENTS

Characterization and simile. Once again Jurgis is the victim of "ruthless economic laws," of fate meted out without regard for human need or virtue. Good fortune, like the bad, comes by chance: it is *luck not pluck* that counts. While Aniele judges Jurgis severely for his mistakes, Marija and Elzbieta decide on a policy of tolerance, successfully urging Jurgis to think of the survivors. To describe Elzbieta, Sinclair uses one of his most naturalistic similes: she is "like the angleworm, which goes on living though cut in half."

Muckraking. The action, as usual, provides Sinclair with numerous opportunities to point out abuses in the economic system: the packers hire "spotters" to deprive Chicago's blacklisted men of work even in distant cities; employment agencies run fake ads in the papers allegedly offering jobs but actually trying to get paid fees in advance; the streetcar company bribes the city council.

Techniques and process. Sinclair also returns to his naturalistic concern with method. He describes the harvester company's ways of dealing with employees as more humane, more paternalistic (although just as arbitrary about sudden closings). Sinclair describes their mass-production techniques in detail, for example, how a certain machine converts rods into bolts. Even this best of places relies on the speed-up, leading Sinclair to say sarcastically, "If we are the greatest nation the sun ever shone upon, it would seem to be mainly because we have been able to goad our wage-earners to this pitch of frenzy."

Chapter 21

PLOT DEVELOPMENT

Again Sinclair unfolds his action by ebb and flow. After the dashing of Jurgis' hopes at the harvester plant, he has trouble finding a new job. The only money he has is what the children bring in, and their fortunes ebb too: Vilimas is threatened with the truant officer, Kotrina by a child molester. It is the children's scavenging in garbage dumps for food that attracts the attention of a settlement worker who gets Jurgis a job in the steel mills: he is hired to move molten rails with a crowbar. But one day he burns his hand when he helps injured men. He is "laid up for eight working days without pay."

Sinclair repeats his motif of how a workingman can see his children regularly only when he is home sick. Jurgis is proud of little Antanas. Back at work full of "plans and dreams," Jurgis comes home one night, wading through deep rainwater which has turned the street "into a canal," and finds a crowd in front of Aniele's house. Antanas has drowned in the "canal."

NATURALISTIC ELEMENTS

Characterization. Again, Sinclair gives us a striking picture of a child. Antanas is "tough . . . nothing could hurt him." He loves to hear the comics read aloud, and he makes up new stories by combining old ones. But he is one more victim of a world in which *fate is determined not by character or strength but by overwhelming amoral forces.*

Sinclair continues too to excel in creating convincing "walk-on" characters. The settlement worker, wearing a fur around her neck, weeps in Aniele's attic when she hears Elzbieta's story of the family's plight. She smiles through her tears that her fiancé will get Jurgis a job in the steel mills or "he will never marry me." Even in jest, her remark reminds us of the naturalistic view of the relationship between sex and economics. In one respect, she is using her power just as Connor used his.

Muckraking. The chapter abounds in Sinclair's endless examples of social evils. Streets are not paved in poor neighborhoods. A steelworker who burns his hand on the job is laid off without pay. Streetcar lines are so designed that "one had to pay two fares" to get wherever he wants to go.

Survival techniques. Typical of the Zolaist stress on techniques for survival is Sinclair's recounting how raking for food in the garbage dumps is more profitable in freezing weather because then the food is better preserved. But the most impressive processes in the chapter are those related to steel making. Again Sinclair contrives to take us on a "tour": a timekeeper takes Jurgis through the mill in an effort to find a foreman who needs "another unskilled hand." Hence we get a panoramic view of huge machines that make the steel and shape it into various products. Sinclair uses his full *metaphoric powers* here. The building housing the Bessemer furnaces is likened in detail to a "big theater": "it was like standing in the center of the earth, where the machinery of time was revolving." An ingot being

worked into a rail becomes "a great red snake escaped from pur-
gatory."

Chapter 22

PLOT DEVELOPMENT

The ebb and flow of Jurgis' fortunes and moods after Antanas'
death is recounted in alternating scenes and narrative summaries. Jurgis flees Aniele's attic, where Antanas lies dead; obeying
"a wild impulse," he hops a freight train going into farm country.
For three years now in Chicago he has rarely "seen a tree," and
now, for the first time since he left Lithuania, he is able to
immerse himself entirely in water — in a stream. Some farmers
feed him, for money or in exchange for his doing chores; but
when one turns him away as a "tramp," Jurgis uproots some of
the man's freshly planted trees. He associates with professional
tramps — most of whom had found that working for a living was
"a losing fight" — and with migratory workers. After a session
with a prostitute, Jurgis falls prey to his conscience; after an
evening spent watching a farm couple bathe their baby, Jurgis
falls prey to "the ghosts of his old life."

CHARACTERIZATION

Effect of environment. The change in his environment restores
Jurgis to physical health and rescues him from the intense
monotony and narrowness of city life. This effect on a character
of a change of surroundings is, of course, a *naturalistic theme*;
but here it also coincides with a *romanticist attitude*: the city
dries up the soul, while Nature replenishes it.

Symbolism. Sinclair signals changes in Jurgis' character with
two major symbolic actions. His bathing in a country stream is *a
ritual of baptism*, the beginning of a new life as he washes away
the old. His uprooting the trees is *a symbolic rehearsal for
rebellion*, signifying his new intention to fight back.

Minor characters. As always, Sinclair proves his ability to represent "walk-on" characters as distinctive persons. One is a farmer with whom Jurgis discusses seasonal employment policies ("When you get through working your horses this fall, will you turn them out in the snow?"). The farmer is open-minded and seems willing to learn even from a tramp. But in *The Jungle* Sinclair is always at his best in describing children, and here he gives us a full description of a baby delighting in its bath. Love of children, who are still "natural" and uncorrupted by civilization, is another romantic theme.

NATURALISTIC TRUTH AND MUCKRAKING

Sinclair gives us a full account of another subject avoided in traditional, genteel literature. Organized groups of prostitutes, "handled by agencies," follow migratory workers from farm harvest to lumber camp to construction site.

Chapter 23

PLOT DEVELOPMENT AND THEME

Structure. The very pattern of the action illustrates Sinclair's *naturalistic theme that in our society, a man's life is a series of ups and downs caused mainly by outer forces.*

Contrasts. Fall weather forces Jurgis back to the city, where after months of cleanliness in the open air, he is plunged into weeks of filth in dark work underground. He helps dig tunnels, ostensibly for telephone conduits, until his arm is broken by machinery. A second, more ironic contrast: his rest in the hospital gives him his "pleasantest Christmas he had had in America." But when he is discharged with a weak arm, he must resort to panhandling.

OTHER NATURALISTIC ELEMENTS

Characterization and theme. Jurgis is becoming more class conscious. For example, he sees religion as "part of the established order that was crushing men down." Evangelists, whose meetings homeless men attend to get in out of the cold, represent "the triumphant and insolent possessors" — insolent because they refuse to acknowledge "that all that was the matter with [the poor people's] souls was that they had not been able to get a decent existence for their bodies." As Sinclair sees it, religion holds a man individually responsible for a fate foisted on him by the economic system.

Muckraking. Sinclair dramatizes further the fact that when an employee is injured on the job, the employer has no responsibility. In the hospital, Jurgis is fed "tinned meat, which no man who had ever worked in Packingtown would feed to his dog," meat regularly fed to "soldiers and sailors, prisoners and inmates of institutions." The tunnels Jurgis works on are part of a scandalous venture. Certain companies have bribed the city council to let them secretly build underground freight subways. This will give businessmen a new transport system in place of surface trucking, and thereby crush the teamsters' union.

Survival techniques. Sinclair's naturalistic recording of the struggle for existence leads him to give us the dollars-and-cents details of Jurgis' weekly budget. He also explains how tunnels are driven, how professional panhandlers fake injuries, how saloonkeepers see bums as a way to attract business — that is, workers with jobs will often expansively treat workers without jobs to a drink.

Chapter 24

PLOT DEVELOPMENT

Structure and theme. After an introduction summing up Jurgis' self-image — "He had lost in the fierce battle of greed, and so was doomed" — Sinclair develops the chapter in one continuous dramatization.

Chance. The author invokes the Zolaist stress on chance: panhandler Jurgis has the sheer luck to hit the fancy of a young aristocrat who, possibly because he is drunk, takes Jurgis home for supper in his palatial mansion. Chance again: the drunk forgets he has given Jurgis a hundred-dollar bill for the cab fare and sends a servant out to pay it.

Contrast. Sinclair thus contrives to let us see how the upper class lives, for the rich boy is the scion of the Jones family, meat packers! The Jones mansion contains vast halls, great staircases, domed ceilings, a marble swimming pool, art by Cellini, jeweled lamps. As Sinclair gives us the cost of each object, we realize that the Joneses have spent, on just one chair, what they pay a Packingtown worker for ten years of dangerous labor. The rich people's servants, suspecting Jurgis will steal something of value, throw him out as soon as the "drunk lord" falls asleep. Jurgis still has the hundred-dollar bill, at least two months' earnings for an unskilled worker.

CHARACTERIZATION

Sinclair develops character as well as story through ironic contrast. Freddie Jones "understands" Jurgis' troubles because Freddie's father, off to Europe, has left Freddie less than two thousand dollars' spending money! "Up against it myself, ole sport . . . hard ole world . . . nuff to drive a feller to drink." With a bankroll in his pocket — more money than Jurgis has ever seen in his life — Freddie can describe himself as "on the verge of starvation." And when Jurgis says he has worked in the yards, Freddie talks of "labor an' capital, commun'ty 'f int'rests . . . ."

STYLE AND ALLUSION

Here Sinclair gives us a rare display of his talent as a writer of bitter comedy. But again he uses an inappropriate literary allusion. When Jurgis gazes at Freddie, he sees "a beautiful boy, with . . . the head of an Antinous." The allusion comes from Sinclair's not from Jurgis' experience. Antinous is a young aristocrat who is chief among the suitors of Penelope in Homer's *Odyssey*.

Chapter 25

PLOT DEVELOPMENT

Structure. Chapter 25 comprises a major turning point in Jurgis' career. His long-foreshadowed rebellion, his outlawry, begins in earnest. Sinclair develops the chapter racily, alternating scenes and summaries and indulging in plenty of editorializing.

Motivation to crime. Jurgis tries to change Jones' hundred-dollar bill in a saloon, and is deliberately given change of one dollar by the bartender; Jurgis attacks him in a rage and is dragged off to jail. The court prefers the bartender's story just as it had preferred Connor's. So when Jurgis meets Duane in jail, Jurgis is thoroughly disillusioned with "law and order," thoroughly motivated to become an outlaw. He commits a violent holdup with Duane who then introduces him to the world of political graft.

Political corruption. Jurgis works for Scully, Democratic boss, who secretly collaborates with the Republicans to rig an election. Scully dupes a rich Jewish brewer into running for alderman simply to get the brewer's "campaign money." Scully uses these funds to swing the election for the Republican candidate, actually a minion of Scully's. Jurgis is paid well by Scully to return to Packingtown as a hog-trimmer and to get his fellow workers to vote Republican! Chicago hails the "Republican" victory as "a triumph of popular government."

CHARACTERIZATION

In his blind rebellion against fate, Jurgis first becomes cynical, in effect joining his corrupt oppressors because he is as yet unaware there is any legal way to fight them. Sinclair tells us of the appearance of a Socialist alternative in the election, but "Jurgis had never got it straight . . . he was content with [the] explanation that the Socialists were the enemies of American institutions."

Ironically, it is his new financial success that develops Jurgis' confidence and even reveals his managerial talents: he herds groups of workers to the polls and passes Scully's money to them to vote "Republican." As Tamoszius said (in Chapter 5), "if you met a man who was rising, you met a knave."

The sinister night watchman (in Chapter 9) is now identified as "Bush" Harper, Scully's right-hand man, a labor spy who has been elected a union leader.

Scully emerges as the master villain. With Sinclair's talent for quick sketches of characters we see just once or twice, he depicts Scully as a shrewd, intuitive observer of people, a man with "rat-like" eyes and "shaking hands." Jurgis is unaware that Scully was to blame for the unpaved street in which Antanas drowned, "had put into office the magistrate who had first sent Jurgis to jail," and was principal stockholder in the real-estate firm that swindled Jurgis' family.

Dapper Duane suddenly goes down to defeat in the "struggle for existence," apparently driven out of town by the police.

MUCKRAKING AND NATURALISM

As plot and characterization indicate, Chapter 25 contains some of Sinclair's most thorough muckraking tirades. The police collect bribes from saloons illegally open on Sundays, and from "madams" running bawdyhouses. Indeed, often a police captain will own the brothel he pretends to be raiding. Duane tells Jurgis that if he becomes known to the police as Duane's partner in crime, he will have to pay off the police to stay out of jail.

Businessmen run the city by bribing party officials with campaign funds, corporation lawyers with fat salaries, contractors with contracts, union leaders with "subsidies," newspapers with advertising. "Tens of thousands of votes were bought for cash." Saddest of all, poor Lithuanian Jurgis — once sent to jail by Callahan, who hates foreigners — is paid to use anti-Semitic arguments in the campaign against the duped Jewish brewer.

Emphasis on processes. In addition to detailing Duane's holdup techniques and the methods of control that businessmen and politicians use to stay in power, Sinclair records at length how "the gigantic Racing Trust" fixes its races and so profits from the poolroom gulls who bet on the horses.

Style, symbolism, and theme. The muckraking passages are journalistic; although the dramatized scenes are spirited, the entire chapter is prosaic by comparison with, say, Chapters 1 and 19. One scene in particular takes on symbolic value. Jurgis worries over the injuries suffered by his first holdup victim: "he never did us any harm." Duane's answer — "He was doing it to somebody as hard as he could" — sums up a naturalistic theme: *in industrial society, man reverts to the law of the jungle.*

Chapter 26

PLOT DEVELOPMENT

Structure: Jurgis' rise to affluence and power is, in true naturalistic fashion, suddenly reversed by an accidental meeting.

Flow and ebb. Staying on in his Packingtown job, Jurgis — on Scully's advice — becomes a "scab" when the Meat Workers' Union calls a strike. As thousands of strikebreakers are imported to replace strikers, Jurgis becomes a boss. Illegally, the strikebreakers are housed in the packing plants, where there are no facilities for even barracks-like living. In these worse-than-prison conditions, Jurgis stumbles one night on Connor, is seized again by his old rage at this man who had ruined his wife and family, and beats Connor on the stone floor until the police knock him out. Jurgis is forced to put up his three-hundred dollars' savings as bond and then to jump bail.

CHARACTERIZATION AND POINT OF VIEW

Once again Jurgis' fate is determined largely by external circumstances. When he sees newspapermen blow a little incident up into sensational "VIOLENCE IN THE YARDS!" he smiles cynically, having lost all faith in the system. Even though he is determined to exploit the falseness of society for his own benefit, and indeed gets "used to being a master of men," he sometimes despises himself. The chance encounter with Connor is actually his salvation; it reminds him which side he should be on, shows him capable still of moral fury.

Racism in the strike. Sinclair's characterization of the strike-breakers is controversial; at best, it is not discreetly handled. Perhaps the problem resides in Sinclair's *confusion of artistic point of view.* We have noted several times that Sinclair describes a scene through Jurgis' eyes yet uses literary allusions (to Homer, for example) that would never occur to Jurgis; it is Sinclair's own point of view that he blends in with Jurgis.' On the other hand, in Chapter 25 Sinclair's account of anti-Semitism figured in the election is well focused, so that we know the jibes at the "sheeny" brewer are the politicians', not Sinclair's.

But in Chapter 26, when Sinclair reports on the racism that figured in the strike, he once again blurs the point of view, just as he does often with literary allusions. He reports how the packers recruit criminals and thugs as strikebreakers, and, as we well know by now, any recent immigrant or other arrival naive enough to be trapped. These include Negroes recently imported from the South. Jurgis, once dupe of Scully's anti-Semitic tactics, now turns his prejudices on these allegedly "stupid black Negroes" who allegedly "did not want to work.'" In expressing the racial aspects of the strikebreaking — the packers obviously knew what they were doing — Sinclair describes "young white girls from the country rubbing elbows with big buck Negroes." Unfortunately, as with his allusions to Wilde and Homer, Sinclair has so confused the point of view that we can read these opinions not as the characters' but as the author's. Since Sinclair has obviously been sympathetic to outcasts from society, like the Lithuanians and the despised working class generally, we cannot actually believe that he himself is racist. But it is unfortunate that this point-of-view carelessness crept into his writing at this point.

LITERARY ALLUSION

Today's reader might be confused by Sinclair's remarks when Jurgis becomes a scab: "So Jurgis became one of the new 'American heroes,' a man whose virtues merited comparison with those of the martyrs of Lexington and Valley Forge. The resemblance was not complete, of course, for Jurgis was generously paid and comfortably clad . . .." Sinclair is making a sarcastic allusion to a remark by Charles W. Eliot, President of Harvard, who had actually compared the scabs with the heroic "martyrs." Eliot glorified the strikebreaker as an example of the finest type of patriot whose liberty had to be guaranteed at all costs. Indeed, in Sinclair's *Appeal to Reason* version of the novel, this passage began: "So Jurgis became one of President Eliot's 'American heroes'...."

TWO VERSIONS OF THE NOVEL

This change is typical of scores of slight emendations that Sinclair made when preparing the serialized version for publication in commercial book format. He also expanded some sections near the end.

Chapter 27

PLOT DEVELOPMENT

Structure. This chapter is divided into three parts: (1) introspection and summary, (2) scene, and (3) introspection and summary.

Scene, accident, and coincidence. Now a fugitive from justice, fearful of being betrayed by anyone he meets, Jurgis returns to street begging. A well-dressed woman he approaches proves to be Alena Jasaityte, "the belle of his wedding feast," who describes herself mysteriously as "not married" but having "a good place." She tells him that Marija also is "doing well." But when Jurgis gets to Marija's "house," the police are raiding it. She tells Jurgis she is supporting Elzbieta and the others on her income as a prostitute, and that if Jurgis had been sensible, "Ona could have taken care of us all" practising that vocation. Tamoszius, she reports, lost a finger on the job, can no longer play fiddle, and has gone away. Stanislovas was accidentally locked in a building and eaten alive by rats. Mistaken for one of the "customers" of the house, Jurgis is taken to jail with other men caught in the raid.

Introspection and summary. Before and after the Marija scene, Sinclair reviews Jurgis' — and the country's — situation through Jurgis' meandering reflections and observations. The strike of twenty thousand Chicago stockyards workers has been smashed, unemployment has been rampant, Jurgis steals food, lines up at "free soup kitchens," and curses that "one hideous accident" — meeting Connor again — that has deprived him of his life as an affluent buccaneer. Now he discovers that not only has *he* been "indecent" but also that Elzbieta's family is living off Marija's "shame."

CHARACTERIZATION AND IRONY

Marija, guardian of the proprieties in Chapter 1, now accepts the fact that *only impropriety succeeds.* She has lost her old energy, seems dull and emotionless, regards everything "from the business point of view."

The meeting with Marija has reawakened long-suppressed emotions in Jurgis, but the chapter ends on the possibility that "the last faint spark of manhood in his soul would flicker out."

OTHER NATURALISTIC ELEMENTS

Truth and documentation. Because prostitution exists, the Zolaist faithfully documents it. Sinclair describes the "house," customers, women, and of course the fact that the raid is caused by the madam's failure to "come to terms" with the police.

Techniques of survival. The Darwinist leanings of naturalistic Sinclair figure again as he describes the ways the unemployed learn to survive, for example, lining up at the bakery to buy stale bread at half-price.

METAPHOR AND IRONY

Sinclair describes Jurgis' varying fortunes in terms of two kinds of prison: "one . . . where the man is behind bars, and everything . . . he desires is outside"; the other "where the things are behind bars, and the man is outside." *Irony* — or saying one thing and meaning another — figures in much of Sinclair's documentation. For example, the new election campaign is under way and "for some reason the people refused to get excited over the struggle."

Chapter 28

PLOT DEVELOPMENT AND NATURALISM

Structure and nature of plot. The *climax* of the novel is brought about, in Zolaist fashion, by sheer chance. But the resolution is anti-Zolaist. The chapter is divided into two parts: the first is Jurgis' last contact with the world of the trapped; the second is his first contact with a world of hope.

"Home." After Marija and the other women are fined, and Jurgis and the other men merely reprimanded by the judge, Jurgis walks "home" with Marija. There he learns that she is addicted to morphine ("If it isn't that, it's drink") supplied by the madam. He promises that he will "go home" to Elzbieta's family. Sinclair's stress on the word home is ironic.

Turning point. Ashamed to face those he once deserted, Jurgis walks the streets instead and chances to find himself outside the "same hall" where he had heard Senator Spareshanks speak the night before. "Bums" often attend political rallies simply to have a place to stay indoors. When the crowd cheers tonight's speaker, Jurgis is cynical. He "had been behind the scenes in politics"; he knew they "were making fools of themselves" — "what had they to do with elections, with governing the country?"

By sheer chance, however, he has stumbled into a Socialist meeting. First he is astonished by the rapt attention — the genuine excitement — of the woman sitting next to him. Then he himself becomes enthralled by the speaker. Sinclair contrives the speech so that it not only sums up Jurgis' situation generally but also touches on recent details of his life. The speaker appeals to people who "work in dangerous and unhealthful places," "toil long hours for another's advantage," are exploited "by organized and predatory Greed," people whose sisters and wives are "driven by hunger to sell their bodies to live." The speech even recalls to us Jurgis' experience in the Jones' mansion: "They live in palaces, they riot in luxury" because the wealth produced by workers and farmers is "poured into their laps." The speaker calls upon the exploited masses to take their fate into their own hands.

Climax. Jurgis' earlier cynicism now drowns in a flood of mixed emotions. On the one hand, he is ashamed that all this time he has allowed himself to be "crushed and beaten," that he has submitted to these horrors, and even repressed the memory of them. On the other hand, he feels a powerful revival of his manhood, his dreams, as though he can still make up for lost time. He is miraculously converted to the speaker's point of view.

Naturalistic documentation. Sinclair provides exact details about the income and expenses of a typical prostitute, Marija, as well as examples of how women are lured or even forced into "white slavery" (or yellow or black — all races are recruited). The Socialist speech, in content and form, is of course straight out of Sinclair's own experience. As William A. Bloodworth says, the speaker combines "the qualities of Eugene V. Debs and George D. Herron," two leading Socialists of the day.

ANTINATURALISTIC CHARACTERIZATION

With Jurgis' discovery of hope, with the revival of his soul and his manhood, *Sinclair says goodbye to pure Zolaism. The naturalistic hero usually goes down to defeat before the forces of circumstance; he does not grow so much as become more and more aware of hopeless closure in his life.* For twenty-seven chapters plus, Sinclair has indeed followed Zolaism. But now he shows that Socialism offers an escape from the naturalistic trap, that man is not a passive resultant of outer forces but can react.

The two main characters in Chapter 28 provide the essential contrast: Marija remains the naturalistic victim, but Jurgis at last becomes an activist.

Chapter 29

PLOT DEVELOPMENT

Structure. The chapter is structured by ebb and flow, but with a new meaning: the ebb-and-flow movement of Jurgis' fortune is now determined not mainly by outer forces but mainly through his own free will.

Flow. Jurgis feels "a new man had been born." He is no longer the sport of circumstances. Most important, "he would have friends and allies."

Ebb. Then he sinks into despair as he realizes he is still a "hobo," ragged, malodorous, with no place to sleep.

Flow. But then he feels that *this* speaker would not despise a man down and out. Jurgis *takes the initiative*, seeking out the speaker and congratulating him! The speaker turns Jurgis over to Ostrinski, a Pole who speaks Lithuanian. In Ostrinski's flat, Jurgis hears about the organization and aims of the Socialist Party, which at that time was a growing third party in America (six years after *The Jungle* appeared, Eugene V. Debs, Socialist candidate for President, would poll nearly a million votes). Jurgis has a place to sleep: Ostrinski's kitchen floor.

CHARACTERIZATION

Jurgis' conversion has influenced his character in several ways. He acquires a new dignity as he takes the initiative and ends his utter loneliness and cynicism. He begins to experience intellectual insights; e.g., that his self-congratulation in Chapter 3 ("I'm glad I'm not a hog!") was pathetic, for "a hog was just what he had been — one of the packers' hogs." They had gotten out of him exactly what they got out of a hog: all the profits possible. He is now part of a movement that will take over the yards "to produce food for human beings and not to heap up fortunes for a band of pirates."

Titles and symbolism. Sinclair sums up the transformation in terms of his title, *The Jungle*. "For four years . . . Jurgis had been wandering and blundering in the depths of a wilderness," but now a hand had "lifted him out of it, and set him on a mountaintop, from which he could survey it all," including the "beasts of prey" that had fallen on him.

Ostrinski. The Polish-American is the first Socialist that Jurgis has paid attention to. He had ignored the ideology of Tamoszius Kuszleika (Chapter 25) and Grandmother Majauskiene (Chapter 6) because he was too harried to be open to ideas. Jurgis is able now to see that although Ostrinski is poor, "what a hero he had been!"

MUCKRAKING AND SOCIALISM

Ostrinski's briefing of Jurgis sums up many of the muckrakers' exposés of the turn-of-the-century years. Employers forced workers to compete for jobs, and so no man could get more than the lowest man would consent to work for; thus the masses lived always on the brink of poverty. Political liberty was a mockery so long as voters were wage slaves. Big Business stole public water supplies, dictated to courts the sentences of dissenting workers, bribed legislators, falsified reports, ruined small businessmen. The Socialist answer was to end private ownership of the means of production, and by peaceful, democratic measures — evolution rather than revolution.

Chapter 30

PLOT DEVELOPMENT

Sinclair contrives Jurgis' political development by exposing him to a series of Socialist leaders and experiences. Jurgis becomes a porter in a hotel owned by a Socialist and frequented by Party members. He learns their arguments and propaganda techniques, acquires the reading habit, and finally, at a Democratic Party meeting, makes a speech from the aisle in which he challenges the Democratic claim that it is always the Republicans who buy the votes. He tells of his own experiences in working for the Democratic boss Scully.

CHARACTERIZATION

Jurgis has come a long way from being the timid immigrant who did not know he had any "rights" except to do as he was told, and from the dupe who served as the cynical minion of Scully.

Several of the characters in this chapter, presented in a series of thumbnail sketches, are modeled on living persons. For example: The "millionaire socialist" — He resembles Gaylord Wilshire who "had made a fortune in business," specifically in billboard advertising, was converted to Socialism, and published a Socialist Party weekly. A "young author" — This is surely Jack London, who "came from California," had been "an oyster pirate," and now "was famous" as author of The Sea Wolf (1904) and other novels, "but wherever he went he still preached the [Socialist] gospel." "A man into whose soul iron had entered" — This is Sinclair himself. It was he who wrote the manifesto "You have lost the strike, and now what are you going to do about it?" The Appeal ran it as a first-page article on September 14, 1904.

Characterization and muckraking. Sinclair continues his muckraking by recounting the experiences of his gallery of Socialists. For example, the hotel owner, Tommy Hinds, had served in the Civil War, in which businessmen had supplied defective guns and shoddy blankets to the Army, at high prices.

LITERARY ALLUSIONS

Tommy Hinds mutters a motto that is his adaptation of a famous phrase by the French philosopher Voltaire (1644 – 1778). Hinds tells Jurgis: "Écrasez l'Infâme!" (Crush the Infamy). By the Infamy, Voltaire had meant the superstition and fanaticism fostered by the Inquisition. By the Infamy Hinds means "Capitalism, my boy."

Sinclair also describes how Hinds "set out upon the trail of the Octopus as soon as the war was over." This is an allusion to Frank Norris' naturalistic novel The Octopus (1901), which dealt with wheat growers and their struggle against the railway magnates.

Chapter 31

PLOT DEVELOPMENT AND DOCUMENTATION

Structure. Sinclair ends his novel by having Jurgis (1) witness an intellectual discussion among Socialists and (2) take part in the 1904 election.

Introductory contrast. In a brief overview of the Lithuanian characters' situations, Jurgis discovers that Marija has resigned herself to her fate as a woman for sale, and Elzbieta is ill and her children "the worse for their life upon the streets." Jurgis however is "the better" because he can "solace himself with a plunge into the Socialist movement."

Platonic dialogue. Just as Plato (427 – 347 B.C.) expounded his ideas in "dialogues," in which a semifictionalized Socrates engages in debate with disciples and other philosophers, so Sinclair further expounds on Socialism by having seven or eight people discuss its nature and its future. Main speakers are an "itinerant evangelist," the Reverend Lucas, and a Swedish ex-professor and food experimenter, Doctor Schliemann. Lucas sees Socialism as the modern version of the teachings of Jesus, "the world's first revolutionist," "himself a beggar and a tramp, an associate of saloonkeepers and women of the town," who repeatedly denounced the rich, doubted they could "enter into . . . Heaven," and indeed himself drove businessmen from the Temple. Schliemann sees Socialism as a step toward anarchism, or a society in which "the end of human existence [is] the free development of every personality, unrestricted by laws."

Schliemann's strongest arguments are similar to Edward Bellamy's *Looking Backward* (1888): that the competitive system produces vast waste of labor, time, materials; that elimination of this waste, use of machinery for public good rather than for private profit, and compulsory work for all would shorten the average person's working day to a fraction of its present length.

1904 election triumph. The novel ends with Jurgis and other Socialists enjoying and discussing the results of the 1904 election, in which Socialists polled over four hundred thousand votes, almost fifty thousand of them in Chicago. A Socialist orator exhorts his comrades to keep up the pressure so that "We shall bear down the opposition . . . CHICAGO WILL BE OURS!"

Autobiographical element. The orator's remarks that conclude the novel are based on a speech that Sinclair himself delivered at a mass meeting in Chicago on Election Day, 1904.

CHARACTERIZATION AND THEMES

Jurgis hardly figures in this chapter, except as someone allied with dedicated people. Effect: whereas most of the novel has been devoted to his *private* agonies and *alienation* from society; now he is happily immersed in a *collective movement* that is daily cultivating his intellect and his sense of human and civic worth. In one sense then, he has rediscovered the happiness he knew in Lithuania, where he had enjoyed *communal* village life.

Apparently Sinclair selects most of his characters for the evening of dialogue to show that the Socialist Party interests a cross-section of 1904 society: Jurgis, a laborer; a female college student; a kindergarten teacher; a clergyman; a philosophical anarchist. The host is not a Socialist but a sympathizer; one guest is an anti-Socialist, an editor who asks why two Socialists could be so different as Lucas and Schliemann. This leading question, of course, allows Sinclair to make his point that Socialism is a democratic movement, directed by discussion among its members, who need agree on only two propositions: (1) the means of production must be publicly and democratically managed; (2) this must be achieved by "class-conscious political organization of wage-earners."

Where are the Ostrinskis? Sinclair's concluding chapter gives the impression that the Socialist Party is dominated by professional people. The "Platonic dialogue" would have been more representative if it included working-class intellectuals like Ostrinski.

LITERARY ASPECTS

Allusions. Chapter 31 abounds in allusions. Schliemann's "mad career" is called a "Mazeppa-ride upon the wild horse Speculation," a reference to Byron's poem "Mazeppa" about a Polish page who rose to become a Tsarist official in the Ukraine but deserted to the service of Sweden. Schliemann alludes to such political philosophers as Friedrich Nietzsche (1844 – 1900) and Prince Piotr Kropotkin (1842 – 1921), but *gives no credit at all to the writer from whom he draws most of his ideas*: Edward Bellamy (1850 – 1898). Bellamy's Utopian novel *Looking Backward* (1888) is an American classic that converted millions to Socialist thinking all over the world.

Style. For several chapters, the literary treatment has become less poetic, less dramatic, less fictional, less psychological and more prosaic, more political, more polemical, more sociological.

DISSATISFACTION WITH THE ENDING

Most critics have found the concluding chapter inferior to the rest of the novel. As a matter of fact, the present (1906) text is not the same as the text published in the Populist-Socialist magazine *One Hoss Philosophy* (October 1905). In that serialized version, Jurgis is arrested on election night (for jumping bail after assaulting Connor). This put Jurgis in the same class as Marija and Elzbieta: perpetually victimized. It had only the literary advantage of making Jurgis a more prominent figure in the final chapter of a novel mainly about *him*. For Sinclair, though, it apparently made the ending too Zolaistic; he wanted to stress the Socialist triumph. So he omitted the arrest in the book version. Jurgis is free physically as well as intellectually at the end.

But this tinkering indicates that Sinclair was probably not secure about his ending. Indeed, in both his *American Outpost: A Book of Reminiscences* (1932) and the updated version, *Autobiography* (1962), Sinclair admits that "The last chapters were not up to standard." He gives as his reasons that "both my health and my money were gone." Leon Harris, in *Upton Sinclair: American Rebel* (1975), says that when Sinclair tried to write the concluding chapters late in 1905, he "found himself paralyzed: for the first time in his life he was unable to write." Sinclair himself sums it up (*Outpost, Autobiography*) by saying, "I did the best I could . . . ."

We shall elaborate on this critical discussion in the chapter "Critical Reputation of *The Jungle*."

Individual Characters
Analyzed

In this chapter, we discuss individual characters in the order of their appearance. For a general discussion of Sinclair's overall techniques of characterization, see the chapter "Overview of *The Jungle*: Story, Themes, Techniques."

Numbers in brackets after a name indicate the chapters in which that character figures or is mentioned. An asterisk (*) after a number indicates the chapter in which that character dies or is reported dead. For a more detailed critical interpretation of a character's action in particular situations, review the appropriate sections in the chapter, "Chapter-by-Chapter Textual Analysis."

Only characters who are given names are discussed here. Even so, this very number — more than sixty — suggests that this is a novel about a large cross-section of society in the time of the action (1900 – 1904).

MARIJA BERCYNSKAS [1 – 6, 8 – 13, 15 – 22, 27 – 28, 31]. Sinclair chooses to open his novel with Marija bustling about in charge of the wedding feast, especially concerned that Lithuanian traditions be observed. Vigorous and strong, although short, she is a female equivalent of Jurgis in this one sense: she believes at the beginning that hard work and faith in the proprieties will be rewarded with security and success. Indeed, she can command higher pay than Jurgis. Her romance with Tamoszius develops her character — and Sinclair's themes — by contrasts and parallels. She can love the petite and frail man for his artistic soul; he learns that for all her surface violence, she is motivated by an inner gentleness. But theirs is one of several love-relations in the novel crushed by the ruthlessness of the economic system. While Jurgis and Ona had to postpone their wedding "into the second year" in America, Marija and Tamoszius are discouraged entirely: alternating unemployment and injuries on the job finally result in their breakup.

Marija suffers the most violent, most negative change of character in the novel. The guardian of proprieties in Chapter 1, she is found, by Chapters 27 – 28, to be living in the conviction that only impropriety pays off. She has taken to prostitution simply because it supports her dependents, "Aunt" Elzbieta and her children. She feels that if Jurgis had accepted Ona's double life, Ona could have saved them all before it was too late. By Chapter 31 Marija is matter-of-factly resigned to her way of life and to the morphine addiction that makes it tolerable.

Sinclair uses Marija as a foil to several other characters. (The term is taken from the jeweler's trade: he will place a sheet of foil behind a gem in order to enhance it or bring out its qualities.) In the early part of the story, Marija's activity contrasts strongly with Ona's passivity; Marija's superior earning power makes Jurgis' male supremacism seem pathetic; she demonstrates in her love for Tamoszius that opposites attract and complement. By the end, when she has changed, she serves as the main foil to the rejuvenated Jurgis. *He has risen above circumstances and taken his fate into his own hands, while Marija has become the classic naturalistic victim, trapped and defeated by forces beyond her control.*

Z. GRAICZUNAS [1]. Owner of the saloon in which the wedding feast is held, he cheats his customers with impunity because he stands in well with local politicians: an early foreshadowing of Sinclair's muckraking.

ONA LUKOSZAITE [1 – 7, 9 – 19*, 20 – 22, 27]. An immigrant from Lithuania at fourteen, married in a harsh new world at six-

teen, dead at eighteen, Ona is the most victimized of all the characters and the one least understood. Small even for her age,
blue-eyed and fair, she seems at the beginning to be passive and
dependent. She accepts Jurgis' decision that she should remain
at home, unlike Marija who works in the outside world; then she,
like him, accepts the fact that economic reverses mean she too
must go to work, even returning to her job too soon after she
bears a child. She also seems to be passive when she yields to the
sexual demands of her boss. Actually, she can be seen as having
made a realistic sacrifice of heroic proportions. She is probably
correct in saying that Connor, her boss, "would have ruined us,"
"I only did it — to save us. It was our only chance."

Indeed, Marija later agrees, telling Jurgis that if he had
accepted Ona's sacrifice, it would truly have been their salvation.
But at first, Jurgis was still too naive, too politically "immature,"
to see that Ona was forced into prostitution the same way he was
forced into humiliating and hazardous work in the fertilizer mills:
by unrelenting economic pressure. Later, in jail, he realizes that
she had suffered "a fate . . . every one knew to be so common."

Sinclair leaves Ona's final agonies mostly to our (and Jurgis')
imagination. Her anguish during Jurgis' imprisonment is only
reported by Stanislovas; her agonies in premature labor are only
heard by Jurgis; until, in the last minutes of her hopeless struggle, we *see* her die.

Sinclair's story of Ona's fate is no exaggeration. Investigations
by other naturalistic writers (Zola, Stephen Crane, Dreiser,
Hardy), by other muckrakers as well as by social scientists and
feminists, have all made it clear that the lower-class woman was
often pressured into some form of sexual slavery by her economic masters.

JURGIS RUDKUS [1 – 31]. In one of two footnotes in the novel,
Sinclair tells us to pronounce the name Yoorghis. *He is the only
character who figures in every chapter: the character through
whose eyes, ears, growth and memory we experience most of the
action. For most of the novel, Sinclair depicts Jurgis as a
Zolaist protagonist: the victim of circumstances, a product of
determinism, of outer forces. But Sinclair resolves the story by*

*having Jurgis grow into an active, free-willed protagonist, a per-
son who finds a philosophy that explains his predicament and
gives him a way out of it.*

A recent immigrant from Lithuania, Jurgis is big, powerful,
strong-faced with black hair, black eyes and beetle brows, but
shy in social affairs (not only in Chapter 1, but still in Chapter
31!). *He believes in the work ethic to the point of naiveté.* His one
answer to any setback is: "I will work harder." Other Chicago
workers cannot dent his confidence that his towering physique
and willingness to do as he is told will guarantee his survival and
success.

Jurgis, then, is also an example of the naif: a literary device
used by an author to help him illustrate the evils of society that
lie in wait for the unwary. (Other good examples are Voltaire's
protagonist in *Candide* and Twain's in *Huckleberry Finn.*) The
naif starts out innocent, trusting the system. Thus he draws unto
himself all types of contemporary evildoers who thrive by
exploiting others. He must learn the truth the hard way. The literary intention is that the reader also will learn how to distinguish illusion from reality. Sinclair uses his naif in an effort to
convince readers that capitalist democracy is a fraud, a contradiction in terms.

Step by step, Sinclair chronicles his naif's disillusionment. Jurgis learns that no laborer can make enough to support his family:
he must send wife and children out to work and still remain part
of "the working poor." He discovers that workers are worn out
by a "speed-up" system and that they are not compensated for
illnesses or injury incurred from the very nature of their work.
Investing money in a house and labor in his job gets a worker no
equity in either. Positions of power tend to go only to the corrupt. Bribes and kickbacks are as common as unemployment and
job insecurity. He finally realizes that even a physically strong
man, willing to work hard, can be beaten by the system; indeed,
the system must defeat and discard him as part of its "progress"
through exploitation of people for profits.

Jurgis' life includes a few bright moments. Becoming a father
deepens his emotions and even induces philosophical reflections
on the meaning of life. But ironically, he is free to enjoy the company of his son only when he is laid off from work. In just a few

years, he is brutalized by circumstances: he no longer enjoys a prepossessing physique but looks seedy and wretched. He acts dull and beats young Stanislovas into going to work.

In a typical, short-lived revival of confidence, he becomes noble and self-sacrificing in adversity. Rather than see his dependents suffer worse privation, he takes the most dangerous, most humiliating job of all: he becomes a fertilizer worker and comes literally to earn the nickname "The Stinker."

His nobility has its limits. Discovering that Ona has been forced by Connor her boss into sexual slavery, Jurgis cannot see that his wife's sacrifice has been greater than his, that hers is a matter of similar degradation by inescapable circumstances. Only after he has beat Connor and gone to jail does he realize that she too had suffered "a fate . . . every one knew to be so common," that she had indeed yielded to save the jobs of all the members of the family subject to Connor's power.

After Ona's death in premature childbirth, after their son's death by accident while his father was at work, Jurgis takes to the country as a tramp. *His physical rejuvenation in the open air is one of the novel's major examples of the Zolaist stress on the effect of changes in environment.* He performs two *symbolic acts*: his bathing in a stream is a *ritual of baptism*, of casting off the old self and taking on a clean new self; his uprooting of a selfish farmer's newly planted trees is a *symbolic rehearsal for rebellion.*

Driven back to the city by winter, he becomes increasingly class-conscious — for example, seeing religion as "part of the established order that was crushing men down," discovering, on a tragicomic visit to the palatial home of a packing tycoon, how the upper class live. After attacking a man who cheats him, Jurgis once again is judged by a magistrate who believes the side of the story told by the more powerful person (first Connor, now Jake the "well-known" pugilist-bartender) and loses all faith in "law and order."

Thus, Sinclair has thoroughly motivated Jurgis' first phase of active rebellion: he drifts into crime and corrupt political work. Available now as assistant to a robber or to a political boss rigging an election, he is now as much for hire as was Ona, but cynically so. Ironically, under these evil auspices, he discovers new confidence and a talent for management. During the 1904 meat packers' strike, he becomes a scab and then a typical boss, driving his workers and taking bribes.

A chance encounter with Connor proves to be Jurgis' moral salvation. Arrested again for furiously beating his wife's seducer, he realizes he must jump bail. But he has proved himself capable once more of moral fury, and he realizes bitterly which side he is really on.

At the climax of the novel, he stumbles into a Socialist meeting. He is profoundly moved by an orator who describes the life of the working class and how workers can take active measures to improve society. Briefly Jurgis experiences guilt that he has submitted for so long to such exploitation as the speaker describes. Then Jurgis realizes that he is entitled to join this movement. "A new man had been born." He was no longer an isolated victim of circumstances; "he would have friends and allies."

In this second phase of his reaction against the Establishment, he is no longer destructive and cynical, but constructive, humanitarian, optimistic. He acquires a new, genuine dignity, as contrasted with his immoral self-confidence during his criminal career. He is reading voraciously, speaking up at meetings, sitting in on high-level intellectual discussions, happily immersed in a growing political movement.

In the last five chapters of the novel Jurgis is contrasted with Marija. She has become the total victim of circumstances that she no longer has the strength to fight: she has prostituted herself, matter-of-factly, to support her relatives. Jurgis has also made a similar descent into Hell, but he has climbed out again, using his new knowledge of evil for moral purposes.

TETA (Aunt) ELZBIETA LUKOSZAITE [1 – 7, 10 – 11, 13 – 17, 20 – 22, 26 – 28, 30 – 31]. Sinclair sees Ona's stepmother, Elzbieta, as one of the immigrants' main contacts with their Old World past and as a means of contrast. It is she who holds the hat at the wedding feast for the donations during the ceremonial dance. Indeed, it was she — along with Dede Antanas — who wanted the wedding postponed until circumstances would permit a proper nuptial party. And when Jurgis announces there is no money for a formal funeral for Elzbieta's little Kristoforas, it is Elzbieta who thinks Ona's father could "rise up out of his [European] grave to rebuke her" for her acquiescence to this violation of tradition; it is Elzbieta who begs and borrows the money for a mass, a hearse, a plot, a wooden cross. Her strong Mother Earth instincts come to the fore again when she sides with Marija, in opposition to Aniele, in forgiving Jurgis for his harsh treatment of Ona so long as he goes back to work for the survivors.

In the earlier portions of the novel, she is a housewife, caring for six children; but after Kristoforas dies, she, too, goes to work in Packingtown. This situation gives Sinclair another way of characterizing industrial work, for Elzbieta, quite familiar with hard domestic work, is still shocked into stupefaction by the furious stultifying pace and monotony of industrial labor. "She was part of the machine she tended, and every faculty that was not needed for the machine was . . . crushed out of existence." Her power for survival evokes one of Sinclair's best similes: she is "like the angleworm, which goes on living though cut in half. . . ."

She goes down to defeat at the end, sick most of the time, dependent on the wages of sin brought in by Marija who herself is ill.

KOTRINA LUKOSZAITE [1, 12 – 14, 17, 19, 21]. Sinclair introduces us to her as she is "staggering beneath a . . . burden" of a "great platter of stewed duck" at the wedding feast. Perhaps this is her happiest moment, and the "burden" ironically symbolic. We see her again screaming for help when Kristoforas has convulsions. At the age of thirteen, she is "prematurely made old" when she takes her mother's place tending the younger children and feeding the wage earners. From Stanislovas we learn that finally, she, too, is driven out to sell newspapers. She is threatened by a child molester, but becomes the leader of the children of the streets.

GRANDMOTHER MAJAUSKIENE [1, 6, 18]. Wrinkled and

maybe eighty, she has survived in the row of houses, where Jurgis' group "buys" a shack, only because her son is a skilled worker and "had sense enough not to marry." A vigorous Socialist, she treats the Rudkus household to the inside story of the real-estate swindle. Her account of the rapid turnover of "buyers," all dispossessed for skipping a "mortgage" payment, foreshadows the fate that awaits Jurgis' family. Along with her zealous class-consciousness she manifests enjoyment over being the one able to reveal these horrors to a house full of innocents. She becomes a fearsome symbol to her tortured listeners, "typifying" fate as she croaks "like some dismal raven."

TAMOSZIUS KUSLEIKA [1, 5, 8, 10 – 12, 16, 25, 27]. He is one of several spirited characters who go down to Zolaist defeat under pressure of the "ruthless laws" of industrial economics. Petite and frail, he is a passionate amateur musician by night, a folder of hides by day, a Socialist. But like Grandmother Majauskiene, he is unable to influence Jurgis politically. At the wedding feast he falls in love with Marija. In Zolaist fiction, love is a trap, and what is a "great adventure" for Marija makes Tamoszius a "victim." Since Marija contributes heavily to the expenses of the Rudkus household, he gets involved and is "doomed to be dragged down too." Their marriage is put off and then, when he loses a finger on his job, he can no longer play fiddle, and like Jonas, he disappears.

VALENTINAVYCZIA [1]. He is a fat round cellist who plays the foreboding "broom, broom" notes at the wedding feast.

DEDA ANTANAS (Grandfather Anthony) [1 – 7*, 9, 14]. Along with Elzbieta, he is the family's main contact with Old World life. He persuaded his son Jurgis to postpone his wedding to Ona until it could be staged properly. In his life in the forests of Lithuania, he had learned that his health was good if he worked outdoors. In Chicago he is first shocked to discover that people of his age are not usually employable; then to learn that he can indeed get a job only if he "kicks back" one third of his earnings to the boss; finally, to realize that his job includes the sweeping of garbage into the meat vats. Working in a cold damp cellar, on a floor wet with acids, he develops consumption as well as sores on his feet and dies in misery. We remember him mainly for his proud insistence on being allowed to work, his refusal to retire, his fierce independence going down to defeat in a harsh New World.

JOKUBAS SZEDVILAS [1 – 4, 6 – 7, 9, 16]. He is a myth in the forests of Lithuania: a man who had emigrated to America and earned a fortune in Packingtown. He is one of the reasons the Rudkus-Lukoszaite families go to Chicago. They find that actually he runs a delicatessen, which he has mortgaged because of "hard times," and he is so poor he must send his twelve-year-old son out to work. He is cynical about real-estate men and the packers, annoying Jurgis as he takes the new arrivals on a tour of the yards. But in close relations with people he trusts, he is vigorously humanitarian; it is he who sees the need to follow up Antanas' sad speech at the wedding with hearty congratulations for the newlyweds, he who contributes several days' earnings to the ceremonial donation.

LUCIJA SZEDVILA [1, 16]. Wife of Jokubas, as fat as he, she helps him run the delicatessen store and describes him as having a "poetical imagination."

ALENA JASAITYTE [1, 27]. Beautiful and proud, she is "the belle of the wedding." She dances like a *grande dame*, and is engaged to Juozas. After he throws her over for another girl, she gets "a good place" in a bawdyhouse. She is Jurgis' means of discovering the whereabouts of Marija.

JUOZAS RACZIUS [1, 27]. A well-paid Durham teamster, he acts like a "tough" at the wedding feast and later jilts the proud Alena.

JADVYGA MARCINKUS [1, 5, 16]. Small, delicate, beautiful but humble, she paints cans to support her mother and sisters; long engaged to Mikolas, she is fond of Ona and inadvertently exposes Ona's lying to Jurgis.

MIKOLAS [1, 15]. A beef boner, he is repeatedly injured on the job, finally loses his hand, and is unable to marry Jadvyga. He is one of Sinclair's many characters who illustrate the fact that turn-of-the century industrialists had little responsibility for workers hurt on the job.

SEBASTIJONAS SZEDVILAS [1]. Hurt by a swinging door at the wedding feast, this three-year-old is consoled by Marija; this gives Sinclair an early chance to characterize Marija as someone who would threaten murder but weep over an injury to a fly.

ANIELE JUKNIENE [1 – 2, 5, 18 – 22, 26]. A sick widow who works hard at several jobs, she is still always on the edge of disaster. She takes in washing, keeps chickens who are fed from garbage heaps, and runs a boarding house for foreigners that presents the newcomers with one of their first insights into the real conditions of immigrants in the land of promise. When pregnant Ona and the other women are dispossessed during Jurgis' first imprisonment, Aniele takes them back into her crowded, verminous house. But after Ona's death, she speaks scornfully of Jurgis' conduct and threatens his group with eviction if he doesn't "pay her some rent." The street in front of her house, neglected by the city because it is a slum area, is the scene of young Antanas' drowning in a deep puddle. In every respect, she serves Sinclair as an extreme example of the fate of the hard-working poor in industrial America.

DURHAM [1, 3, 5 – 7, 9 – 13, 16, 18, 20]. Owner of one of the giant meat-packing plants, "old man Durham" is supposed to have sent "agents into every city and village in Europe to spread the tale of the chances of work and high wages at the stock-yards." This gives him a steady supply of cheap labor and scabs, and makes it easier to preclude the union's staging any successful strike. We never see him; he is part of the sinister upper class that is talked about in whispers.

BROWN [1 – 4, 7, 10, 12, 20, 26]. Another owner of a giant packing plant, he is seen by Sinclair as one of the cruel capitalists making profits by overworking his employees, discarding them as soon as they are hurt or "broken" on the job, and bribing politicians and courts to run Chicago for the benefit of businessmen.

OLD MAN JONES [1, 8, 24, 26]. He is the only one of the three Beef Trust tycoons (see Durham and Brown) that we ever come close to. We meet his idle son and visit his palatial home, where each member of the Jones family enjoys a private apartment larger than the entire house into which Aniele crowds twenty-five poor people.

JONAS LUKOSZAITE [2, 4 – 6, 9, 11 – 12, 14, 20]. It was Jonas (Elzbieta's brother) who suggested that the Rudkus-Lukoszaite families go to Chicago because his friend Jokubas had gotten "rich" in Packingtown. He gets dangerous work pushing a hand truck (his predecessor had been crushed by it). But like Tamoszius, he finds that his earnings are being sucked into the upkeep of the house. He pays good board but must live in a family where nobody gets enough to eat. "Not in the least like a hero," he takes off on his own. He serves as another illustration of how only the unmarried worker is free and mobile in the industrial world.

STANISLOVAS LUKOSZAITE [4, 6 – 7, 11 – 12, 15, 17, 27*]. He is perhaps Sinclair's main illustration of industrial society's cruel treatment of children. At first he is able to take advantage of the opportunity in America to go to school. But the family's financial reverses force them to send him to work at the age of fourteen; he becomes a machine tender in an unheated cellar. After one of his young co-workers loses his ears to frostbite, Stanislovas develops a terror of winter and has to be punched into going to work. He loses his job as part of Connor's revenge on Jurgis, and he joins his younger brothers and Kotrina selling papers on the streets. Drunk on beer, he falls asleep in an oil factory, is locked in at night, and eaten alive by rats.

MARY DENNIS [5]. A can painter who supported her child, she became ill and, although she had fifteen years' service, was summarily fired when Marija applied for a job.

THE LAFFERTYS [6]. One of the families who preceded Jurgis' household as owners of the "new" house.

TOMMY FINNERGAN [8] He is a good example of Sinclair's ability to sketch a character who appears just once. Tom spends his life trying to make some "strange experience" with "shperrits" understandable to his fellow unionists.

"BUSH" HARPER [9, 25 – 26]. We see him first as a sinister, anonymous "night-watchman" at Brown's who pays Jurgis to be naturalized so that he can also get paid to vote Brown's way. When Jurgis joins the underworld, he meets Harper again. Harper sends him to Scully to be assigned as a well-paid political worker under the guise of a hog trimmer. Bush not only arranges for Jurgis to go free on bail after his second assault on Connor, but Bush pockets the bail. He is one of Sinclair's characters dramatizing the link between Big Business and politics.

MIKE SCULLY [9, 21, 25 – 27, 30]. He is a composite figure of the corrupt political bosses that muckrakers like Lincoln Steffens and Sinclair were exposing at the time. A cunning man with ratlike eyes, who sizes up people fast, he controls Chicago by buying votes and rigging elections. He gets the necessary money by taking bribes from criminals and business men and drawing the pay of dead civil service workers. He is principal stockholder in the real estate firm that swindles Jurgis out of his row house. It is Scully who gives Jurgis the letter that gets him work in

Packingtown as a cover for corrupt political work and Scully who advises Jurgis to become a scab.

MISS HENDERSON [10, 15, 17]. Ona's "forelady," she lives in a bawdyhouse with Ona's boss Connor and recruits prostitutes from the packing plants, especially when they "lay off" workers. She has the "temper of a hyena" and can be heard arguing with a former lover, the superintendent, who presumably has given her her job to "keep her quiet." She especially hates married women — out of jealousy? — and Ona sees this as one of the reasons Miss Henderson plotted to supply Ona for Connor's pleasure. She is one of Sinclair's characters illustrating the way industrial leaders use their economic power to force female workers into sexual slavery.

PHIL CONNOR [10, 15, 17 – 18, 25 – 26]. Not until late in the novel does Jurgis learn that Connor is "one of Scully's biggest men." Connor forced Ona to become his mistress simply by threatening to have Ona, Jurgis, Marija, and Elzbieta fired: in short, to ruin the family. This is exactly what he does anyhow after Jurgis thrashes him. *Ironically, Connor becomes a means to Jurgis' salvation.* When Jurgis beats up Connor a second time, it ends Jurgis' life in the world of corrupt politics and criminal strikebreaking; it makes him realize which side he really belongs on. Connor is Sinclair's main example of businessmen's alliance with politics and prostitution.

ANTANAS RUDKUS [10, 11, 14, 18, 20– 21]. Like Stanislovas, little Antanas exemplifies Sinclair's view of how industrial America treats working-class children. An enormous child, he is the "living image of his father." Since his mother must return to work soon after his birth, he is fed on the "pale blue poison that was called milk at the corner grocery," and he never gets enough to eat. Motherless, his father off to work, he one day falls off the sidewalk — that is, from a platform of wooden boards — into the unpaved street — which is to say, into a puddle so deep it "turned into a canal" — and he drowns.

VILIMAS LUKOSZAITE [12 – 13, 21, 31].

NIKALOJUS LUKOSZAITE [12 – 13, 31]. The family's poverty forces them to send Vilimas, eleven, and Nikalojus, ten, out to work as newsboys. Sinclair says sarcastically that "there was no reason why their family should starve when tens of thousands of children no older were earning their own livings." And so before they are teenagers, the boys learn how to cheat the streetcar conductor, where they can sleep in doorways, which places are bawdyhouses and which are saloons. By the end of the novel, they exemplify Zola's stress on the effect of environment. They are "wild and unruly, and very much the worse for their life upon the streets."

KRISTOFORAS LUKOSZAITE [13*]. Three-year old child of Elzbieta, he dies of convulsions after eating tubercular pork. He is Sinclair's extreme example of the bad effect of adulterated food on immigrants raised on natural food in Europe.

PAT CALLAHAN [16 – 17]. He began his political career by drawing simultaneous pay for two full-time city jobs. Owner of dives and brothels, he is the magistrate who judges Jurgis' case of assault on Connor. Jurgis tells the truth, and Connor a batch of lies, but Callahan believes Connor. The linkage between business, justice, and prostitution elicits from Sinclair one of his best metaphors: "If Scully was the thumb, Pat Callahan was the first finger of the unseen hand whereby the packers held down the people."

JACK DUANE [17, 25 – 28]. A dapper, well-educated electrical engineer, Jack becomes disillusioned with "law and order" when he is robbed of a major invention "by a great company" that makes a fortune on it. Now a criminal with a prison record, he introduces the awed and also disillusioned Jurgis to the world of holdup men and corrupt political workers. He is Sinclair's extreme example of a competitive society's "dog eat dog" philosophy. "It is a case of us or the other fellow," he tells Jurgis, "and I say the other fellow every time."

MRS. OLSZEWSKI [18]. Wife of a skilled butcher, she can afford to contribute half a dollar to Jurgis' fund for a midwife.

MADAME HAUPT [19, 21]. She is perhaps the best example of Sinclair's ability to draw colorful portraits of people who figure briefly in his action. A midwife, she is a gross woman, living in filth, eating cheap food, but someone whose sense of responsibility can be invoked. Her usual fee for a delivery is $25, but she finally agrees to accept Jurgis' $1.25 as a down payment. Working all night in Aniele's attic, "a place vere it is not fit for dogs to be born," she finally gives up, losing child and mother amid curses for people who "leave [Ona] to kill herself" when she might have been "vell and strong, if she been treated right."

JUOZAPAS LUKOSZAITE [13, 21]. He is one of Elzbieta's two crippled children. It is his raking the garbage heaps for food that attracts the attention of a settlement worker who gets Jurgis his job in the steel works. He serves Sinclair as a *link in a naturalistic chain of causation.*

FREDERICK ("Freddie") JONES [24 – 25]. The son of "Old Man Jones," the packing tycoon, he provides us with Sinclair's most sustained, most bitterly comic satire. Approached by panhandler Jurgis for a handout, the drunk eighteen-year-old heir to the Jones fortune is totally incapable of understanding Jurgis' plight except in terms of his own. For example, when Jurgis says "I've got no money, sir," Freddie understands: "—jess like me? No money, either — a'most busted." By this he means he has only several hundred dollars of pocket money to last "till the first." The wad of bills Jones takes out to find cab fare is "more money than Jurgis had ever seen in his life before." Taking Jurgis home to dinner, Jones is oblivious to Jurgis' real sufferings as he takes the seedy panhandler on a tour of his father's palatial mansion. Hearing that Jurgis has worked in the yards, Freddie says his father would be "glad to see you. Great fren's with the men . . . labor an' capital, commun'ty 'f int'rests . . . ." It's clear that Freddie has no real understanding of capital-labor relations, or of the way the "Old Man" has acquired his fortune. During Freddie's talk, the reader — if not Jurgis — can see that the Old Man's greed has brought his family no real happiness. Freddie's relatives apparently are living a loveless life, wallowing in banal materialism, with Freddie himself already a confirmed alcoholic.

If Freddie has no appreciation of differences in economic class, his servants do (see Hamilton). Suspecting that Jurgis will steal — almost anything in reach would feed, house and clothe Jurgis for a year — the butler throws Jurgis out at the first opportunity. But he still has the hundred-dollar bill that Freddie had given him to pay the cabbie with; forgetfully, on arriving home, Freddie had sent a servant out to pay the fare. This "accident" of the forgotten hundred-dollar bill is what lands Jurgis in jail again. So, in addition to providing insight into the lives of the rich, the Freddie episode also serves as part of the circumstances leading Jurgis to his descent into Hell: his career as a mugger's helper and a political thug.

HAMILTON [24]. The now stately, now snarling butler of the Jones mansion, he resents having to feed Jurgis and, after "Master Freddie" falls asleep, kicks Jurgis down the steps into the snow.

ADMIRAL DEWEY [24]. The Joneses' monstrous bulldog, he intimidates Jurgis into accepting bad treatment from Hamilton.

JAKE [25]. Crafty bartender, a well-known pugilist, he cheats Jurgis out of ninety-nine dollars when he "changes" Jurgis' hundred-dollar bill.

PAPA HANSON [25]. Owner of the dive where Duane is hiding from the police, he agrees to give Duane sufficient notice of any police raid. This means that Papa works hand-in-hand with the "law" and Duane is safe so long as he bribes everybody.

ROSENSTEG [25]. He is the pawnbroker who buys stolen goods from Duane.

BUCK HALLORAN [25]. A political worker, he engages Jurgis to collect the paychecks of nonexistent city laborers. He is one of Sinclair's many characters who illustrate a political or industrial evil.

GOLDBERGER [25]. "Runner" of a "sportinghouse" (brothel), he shows Duane and Jurgis some of the secrets of dishonest gambling. Through Goldberger, Sinclair effects a mini-exposé of the Racing Trust.

SCOTTY DOYLE [25, 27, 30]. A tenpin setter in a bowling alley, Scotty is the pawn of Scully, "boss" of the Democratic political machine. But the Republicans agree to run Scotty as *their* candidate for alderman so that the Republicans can have the glory while the Democrats have the secret power. The significance in Jurgis' life is this: during his cynical career in crime, he helps Scully rally the workers to vote for Scotty. But after Jurgis becomes a Socialist, his bad conscience makes him want to "undo" his dirty work in the Doyle campaign.

HARMON [25]. He is one of the head managers of Durham's; for political reasons, Scully orders him to give Jurgis a job in the plant.

PAT MURPHY [25 – 26]. He runs the hog-killing room at Durham's where Jurgis gets a job in order to influence Packingtown workers to vote for Doyle.

SENATOR SPARESHANKS [27]. At one of the political meetings that panhandler Jurgis attends, simply to get some rest indoors, the "eloquent" and corrupt Senator is the speaker. He serves as Sinclair's means of satirizing the high tariff.

POLLY SIMPSON [27 – 28]. Stout, painted-cheeked madame, her bawdyhouse is raided because she hasn't "come to terms" with the police. She is one of several characters Sinclair uses to show the intimate relations between crime and "the law."

WALTERS [29]. Big bespectacled man, he tries unsuccessfully to keep Jurgis from seeing the Socialist leader; he turns Jurgis over to Ostrinski. Through Walters, Sinclair shows us how concerned the great leader's (Debs'?) associates are that he is exhausting himself.

OSTRINSKI [29 – 30]. Comrade Ostrinski is a good example of Sinclair's ability to depict in depth a character we know for only a brief time. He is revealed to us as a man so physically unprepossessing — ugly, lame, wizened, grotesque — that he has to win us over by his nobility of character and his devotion to ideas. Although he and his wife work twelve or fourteen hours a day as "pants finishers," they can barely keep alive on the proceeds. Their hope is sustained by their devotion to the Socialist cause. Sitting "tilted back in his stiff kitchen chair," Ostrinski tells Jurgis all about the conditions that have fostered the Party. "As fast as the unions were broken up," when industrialists crushed their strikes, that fast "the men were coming over to the Socialists." They were campaigning for the time when "the working class should go to the polls and seize the powers of government, and put an end" to private ownership of the means of production.

This scene is also a good example of Sinclair's ability to reveal one character through the eyes of another. "To Jurgis [Ostrinski] seemed . . . a wonderful person . . . poor, the lowest of the low, hunger-driven and miserable — and yet how much he knew, how much he had dared and achieved, what a hero . . .!"

TOMMY HINDS [30 – 31]. Comrade Hinds is another character that Sinclair manages to make lively in a swift thumbnail sketch. Squat and broadshouldered, jolly but determined, Tommy learned about corrupt businessmen and political graft when he had to fight in the Civil War with "rotten muskets" and shiver under "shoddy blankets." His career gives Sinclair a chance to review the course of left-wing politics in the period 1865 – 1904. Tommy hires Jurgis as porter in the Hinds Hotel, a "very hotbed of . . . propaganda," whose lobby is the scene of continual political debate. Here Jurgis learns that what is usually prized as "individualism" in America means that "tens of thousands . . . herd together and obey the orders of a . . . magnate, and produce hundreds of millions of dollars of wealth for him."

AMOS STRUVER [30]. As a farmer he had fought the railroads and other trusts and is now clerk at Tommy Hinds' Socialist hotel.

HARRY ADAMS [30 – 31]. Assistant clerk at the Hinds Hotel, he once organized a strike in South Carolina and was jailed by "a judge who was a cousin of the mill owner with whose business" Adams had "interfered." Sinclair uses Adams' experiences to show again the corrupt relations between business and the law.

FISHER [31]. Chicago millionaire, he sympathizes with the Socialist Party and lives in the slums to do social work with the poor and oppressed.

MAYNARD [31]. A magazine editor hostile to the Socialist cause, he is a guest at Fisher's; he questions the Socialists in a way that allows Sinclair to develop some of his major points.

LUCAS [31]. An itinerant evangelist, he sees the Socialist Party as carrying on the work of Jesus of Nazareth.

NICHOLAS SCHLIEMANN [31]. A Swede, an ex-professor of philosophy, an experimenter with diet, he hopes for a Socialist victory as the first step toward the establishment of an anarchist society, that is, a society with no restraints at all on individual freedom so long as no one exploits any one else. Schliemann is one of a dozen or so characters that Sinclair introduces to show that *the Socialist Party includes people of many diverse backgrounds and beliefs.* This is important since Sinclair is trying to demonstrate that the Socialist Party would, upon gaining political control, continue to develop the country in a democratic manner.

Critical Reputation
of THE JUNGLE

With its muckraking, its Zolaism, and its Socialist Party conclusion, *The Jungle* was destined to provoke controversy, both political and literary. Unfortunately, in the early years of the book's career, many critics were influenced in their literary judgment by their political convictions. Only with time have critics generally been able to arrive at more balanced, more objective views of *The Jungle*.

EARLY RECOGNITION BY WRITERS AND SOCIALISTS

When *The Jungle* ran serially in the Socialist *Appeal*, it reached probably half a million readers (the audited circulation was 260,000, according to *Ayer's Annual*; we can assume that each copy was read on the average by more than one person). The excitement generated among ordinary readers is evidenced by two developments. The Girard, Kansas, office of the *Appeal* had difficulty supplying "back copies" to people who had missed the opening chapters. And President Theodore Roosevelt himself told Upton Sinclair that while the novel was running serially, the White House was receiving an average of a hundred letters a day demanding that the government take action on Sinclair's exposé.

Now this initial audience, as Floyd Dell makes clear, "was of farmers resting in stocking feet beside the stove of winter evenings, and of discontented workingmen in a thousand cities and towns — an audience which . . . understood the truths of human suffering which [*The Jungle*] so vividly portrayed. That was its first success — its recognition and acclaim by a proletarian audience."

The point for us is that *Sinclair had performed the miracle of writing a serious work of fiction that had mass appeal for a working-class audience not accustomed to reading serious fiction.* But Sinclair also had some indication from fellow writers that his novel had literary merit as well as mass appeal.

Phillips' admiration. Sinclair received, for example, a letter of praise from the well-known writer David Graham Phillips (1867 – 1911). Phillips' first novel, *The Great God Success*, had appeared in 1901; at the very time that *The Jungle* was running in the *Appeal*, Phillips was preparing his sensational articles on corruption in the U.S. Senate that would appear in *Cosmopolitan* in 1906.

"I never expected to read a serial," Phillips admitted to Sinclair. But "I am reading *The Jungle*, and I should be afraid to tell you how it affects me. It is so simple, so true, so tragic, and so human. I have a feeling that you yourself will be dazed some day by the excitement about it."

This admiration came from a writer whose aims were similar to Sinclair's; Phillips is still discussed in cultural histories as an important author of social problem fiction and nonfiction.

Jack London's praise. Then, when it seemed for a while that Sinclair would have trouble getting *The Jungle* published as a book by a commercial house, the *Appeal* urged its readers to subsidize the work by ordering copies and paying in advance for a "Sustainer's Edition." There is no doubt that this maneuver succeeded largely through the support of the famous Jack London (1876 – 1916). Then thirty, London had already published such classic novels as *The Call of the Wild*, *The Sea Wolf*, *White Fang* and the political tract, *The People of the Abyss*. Now, from the pen of this romantic figure came a rousing "manifesto" published by the *Appeal* as a broadside: "Here it is at last! The *Uncle Tom's Cabin* of wage slavery! . . .. And what *Uncle Tom's Cabin* did for black slaves, *The Jungle* has a very large chance to do for the white slaves of today. . . ." London's literary judgment was that the novel "is alive and warm . . . brutal with life . . .

written of sweat and blood, and groans and tears." London was contrasting it with the "polite" fiction of his day when he added: "It depicts, not what man ought to be, but what man is compelled to be in this, our world in the Twentieth Century. . . . All you have to do is to give this book a start . . . it will run away with you."

London prophesied a great future for *The Jungle*: "The printers will be worked to death getting out larger and larger editions. It will go out by the hundreds of thousands. . . . It will open countless ears that have been deaf to Socialism."

At least the first part of his prediction came true. And his broadside worked: twelve thousand orders poured in for the Sustainer's Edition.

CRITICAL REACTION TO COMMERCIAL EDITION

We are not surprised then to discover that many newspapers for the general (non-Socialist) public ran reviews of the book written in reaction to the Socialist propaganda. They could not ignore *The Jungle* entirely. Indeed the reviews had to be pretty thorough because the novel had figured in the news long before it appeared in its first commercial edition (see the chapter, "Upton Sinclair, Theodore Roosevelt, and Lyndon Johnson"). *The New York Times Book Review* had announced on January 27, 1906, that the novel had been cleared by the lawyer (see Chapter 2) and would appear on February 15; then on February 17 it announced that the final publication date would be February 26. "Editions have already been called for by William Heinemann of London, and also by an Australian firm." Doubleday, Page was exploiting fully the suspense created by its own investigation and by the *Appeal* editions.

Less than a week after the commercial edition appeared, the *Times Book Review* ran a lengthy, detailed attack under these headlines:

JURGIS RUDKUS AND 'THE JUNGLE.' A 'Dispassionate Examination' of Upton Sinclair's Application of Zola's Methods to a Chicago Environment.

The anonymous reviewer began: "Inasmuch as Mr. Upton Sinclair's co-workers in the field of Socialistic propaganda have acclaimed his book as 'a great book' . . .. it becomes the plain duty of the reviewer to examine *The Jungle* with a candid and open mind, that its quality as literature and its efficiency as polemic may be fairly appraised."

While the reviewer found the work "in many ways a brilliant study of the great industries of Chicago," he judged it lacking both as literature and as polemic.

"*As literature.*" As any Zolaist might have predicted, the *Times* chastised Sinclair for telling the truth about the speech of the working class. "The language of the stockyards, as employed by Mr. Sinclair, is often quite unquotable." The reviewer complained that Sinclair's "pictures are not convincing. His work becomes mechanical. . . . The ear continuously catches a false note." He saw the resolution — in which, as he understood it, a crushed, broken, mindless drunkard is miraculously regenerated overnight by Socialist philosophers — as contrived and incredible.

"*Not a great work.*" Sinclair's "realism is often striking," the *Times* conceded: "But he seems to write not from the heart but from the head, with that facile glitter of contrast and exaggeration that is characteristic of the school of young writers that have set out to deliver us from the evils of capitalism."

In other words, the *Times* critic was "skeptical about [Sinclair's] sincerity. His art is too obvious, his devices too trite, and he has too much joy in them." The reviewer's final judgment was that *The Jungle* "is not, after all, a great and epoch-making work."

Zolaism. As the headline made clear, the *Times* critic correctly put Sinclair in the Zolaist camp. It is "evident that he expected his story to be taken as a scientific study of industrial conditions and his characters as 'human documents.' Zola with great solemnity . . . forced upon his readers the scientific aspect of his work. Naturalism was the true method, the scientific spirit . . . ." Zola, the reviewer acknowledged, was "in his way a manifest genius." But Mr. Sinclair "must be . . . set down as merely clever."

Then the *Times* attacked both master and disciple for the "shallowness of the scientific pretensions of both." He voiced a common complaint against the Zolaists: they study "but one aspect, and that the meanest, the most hideous, . . . most vicious and painful of the phases of human life and conduct.. . . Virtue, generosity, good impulses . . . honesty have their place and influence in the stockyard population, no doubt. They do not . . . engage the pen of Mr. Sinclair."

Unfair? Today's reader might see these last comments as especially unfair. The reviewer did not point out that the "meanest, most hideous, most vicious and painful" aspects of life were precisely the ones that the "polite literature" of his day ignored, that it was in reaction to that distortion that the Zolaists stressed these "phases." Further, is it fair to say that "virtue, generosity, good impulses . . . honesty . . . do not engage the pen of Mr. Sinclair"? Isn't Jurgis' early determination, his faith in the work ethic — isn't Dede Antanas' struggle — to be equated with virtue? Isn't Elzbieta's going out to work so the boys can return to school a "good impulse"? Isn't the mortgaged Jokubas' giving to the *veselija* to be seen as "generosity" that engages Sinclair's pen? Perhaps the *Times* reviewer meant that Sinclair did not find many good impulses among the bosses and owners. He tendentiously ignored Sinclair's point that in a society in which Greed rules, good impulses produce losers. In such a society, as Duane and Marija discovered, impropriety really can pay off.

"As polemic." Surely the *Times* writer punched below the belt when he said, "Free love seems to be inseparable from socialism." Was Connor, who pressured working girls into illicit sex, a Socialist? The "agents" who supplied women for migratory workers? The magistrate who owned brothels? Is "free love" an essential part of Sinclair's argument for Socialism? The *Times* also complained that "Socialists assume that the unequal distribution of wealth is the cause of inequality of conditions, quite overlooking the fact that inequality of capacity is . . . important . . . in bringing about the disparity in earthly possessions."

A friend of Sinclair would ask, "Capacity for what — cunning, cruelty, ruthlessness? And how about inequality of opportunity? Did Stanislovas and Kotrina have the same chance to go to school, to loaf and read, that Freddie Jones had?"

Bemused, the reviewer noted that in Sinclair's Socialist society, people would work only one hour a day. "We feel sure that in that ideal system two personages would be forced to work over-time — the devil and the barkeeper." Even in 1906, that argument against reducing the working hours in industry must have been considered "too trite." The student of history, or of "taste," may like to ponder what the *Times* meant by examining *The Jungle* with "a candid and open mind."

"*Immorality.*" The *Times* reviewer reflected a common prejudice against literature that tells the truth, as Sinclair did, about, for example, the arrest of prostitutes who have failed to "come to terms" with the police. On May 21, 1906, *The New York Times* reported, on page one, that the Mechanics Library in New York, having found that parts of *The Jungle* "savored of immorality," that parts were unsuited "for the general perusal of young girls," would issue the book only at the discretion of the librarian.

INTERNATIONAL ACCLAIM

For the time being at least, *The New York Times Book Review* writer and the Mechanics Library officials seem to have been in the minority, and Phillips and London in the majority; for *The Jungle* became a best seller for most of 1906, on both sides of the Atlantic. The *New York Evening World* observed: "Not since Byron awoke one morning to find himself famous has there been such an example of world-wide celebrity won in a day by a book as has come to Upton Sinclair. Yesterday unknown, the author of *The Jungle* is today a familiar name on two continents . . . [and] even in far-off Australia."

Winston Churchill's review. In England, the Honorable Winston Churchill, then a thirty-two-year-old Member of Parliament, published a two-part, five-thousand-word study of *The Jungle* in a new weekly called *P.T.O.* He opened with the observation: "When I promised to write a few notes on this book . . . I had an object — I hoped to make it better known. In the weeks that have passed that object has disappeared. The book has become famous."

Churchill felt that "this remarkable book" might teach a lesson to Englishmen: "The issue between Capital and Labour is far more cleanly cut today in the United States than in other communities." He saw a chance that American writers might provide "answers to many of the outstanding questions of economics and sociology upon whose verge British political parties stand in perplexity and hesitation." That was one reason why "English readers should not shrink from the malodorous recesses of Mr. Upton Sinclair's *The Jungle.*"

A German translation soon appeared, followed by versions in almost every civilized language. But oddly enough, while Sinclair's fame continued to soar all over the world, it suddenly declined in his native land. This contrast is symbolized by the visit to America in 1914 of the great European critic Georg Brandes. Astonished by Sinclair's fall from grace in America, Brandes made it a point to tell reporters: "I find three present-day American novelists worth reading — Frank Norris, Jack London, and Upton Sinclair." Many newspapers quoted the remark omitting the third author! What had happened?

BRIEF SLUMP IN POPULARITY

Several explanations have been offered for the temporary decline of Sinclair's reputation in America. The magazines that had published the muckrakers (such as Phillips in *Cosmopolitan*, Sinclair in *Everybody's*) were threatened by Big Business — which said, in effect, "Change your editorial policy or *lose your advertising.*" And they changed — all but one. *Hampton's* continued to run articles by the muckrakers. But as Harvey Swados writes, B. H. Hampton "awoke one day in 1911 to find that financial control of *Hampton's* . . . had been maneuvered out of his hands and that the magazine was going to be scuttled — apparently by underground agreement of some of the financial interests which had been plagued by its revelations."

And so the very periodicals that had built their huge circulations with muckraking exposés now embarked on a campaign to improve the image of industrial conditions in America. Attacks on Big Business were characterized as unpatriotic, un-American. Meanwhile, President Roosevelt had left the White House in 1909, the "Progressive Era" in politics had ebbed, and Sinclair went into eclipse along with the "Trust Busters" and the muckrakers.

Another simple truth was that one of his two audiences no

longer needed him, politically speaking. His original, working-class audience of course still admired *The Jungle* as a study of horrible working conditions in American industry. But his second, middle-class audience had been more concerned with *The Jungle* as an exposé of the unhealthful condition of their meat supply. Now that the Pure Food Act had been passed, they could be indifferent to Sinclair's other — his main — message. As Sinclair put it so well himself, "I aimed at the public's heart and by accident I hit it in the stomach."

At this point, of course, Sinclair's literary flaws, often overlooked in the political enthusiasm of 1905 – 1906, now stood out more prominently as easy targets for hostile critics, and as facts to be reckoned with even by his friends.

THE JUNGLE BECOMES A CLASSIC

The contrast between Sinclair's reputations in Europe and at home was explained by Floyd Dell in his *Upton Sinclair: A Study in Social Protest* (1927), one of the books that probably turned the tide. In the United States, Dell noted, there was a deep-seated feeling that writers who take sides in politics are not "artistic," not "pure" artists. But England with its Jonathan Swift and France its Voltaire had long traditions of writers fighting against wrong. In Europe, Sinclair was viewed, along with Bernard Shaw and H. G. Wells, as one of these embattled men of letters. Dell urged Americans to take a more European, less purely "literary" attitude toward the author of *The Jungle*. He insisted that we deal with Sinclair's faults as "the faults of a great writer," much as we do when we consider Theodore Dreiser.

A "ragged philosopher." In the same year, Carl Van Doren, in his book on *Contemporary American Novelists*, noted that "the times have furnished Mr. Sinclair the keen, cool, dangerous art of Thomas Paine." And that, Van Doren added, "is to rank Mr. Sinclair with the ragged philosophers . . . rather than with learned misanthropes like Swift or intellectual ironists like . . . Shaw."

Sinclair's "eloquence." Sinclair, said Van Doren, "speaks as a Socialist who has dug up a multitude of economic facts and can present them with appalling force; he speaks as a poet sustained by visions and generous hopes." The general public had seen the plight of the American workers "as something essential to the very structure of society, as Aristotle saw slavery. Mr. Sinclair proclaimed . . . that their plight was not essential; . . . he prophesied the revolution with an eloquence which, though the revolution has not come, still warms and lifts the raw material with which he had to deal."

Brooks' attacks. But the eminent critic Van Wyck Brooks, who could be considered one of the "purists," attacked Sinclair repeatedly. In his *Emerson and Others* (1927) Brooks criticized Sinclair for his rhetorical weaknesses. In *Sketches in Criticism* (1932), he attacked Sinclair's very approach to his art: "Mr. Sinclair says that the incidents in his book are based on fact and that his characters are studied from life. No doubt they are. But Mr. Sinclair, like the rest of us, has seen what he wanted to see" and is guilty of a "special simplification of the social system."

Granting "that nothing has so much meaning as the struggles of the dispossessed," Brooks declared that "the question is how the writer can best aid them." Not, Brooks thinks, by going and living with his characters:

> . . . strange as it may seem, the only way for a writer to aid the dispossessed, *as a writer*, is by preserving his detachment. If he cannot understand the dispossessed without sharing the conditions of their life, he reveals his own incompetence, he reveals a lack of just that intuitive power which justifies his choosing to be a writer. . . . A writer who, in order to understand his characters, has to share their life in its specific actuality is almost certain, sensitive as he is, to react to that life as they themselves react to it, to fall under the sway of the same resentments and passions, and to be limited by the same self-pity that handicaps them. He becomes the "character" — and ceases to be the writer.

In his correspondence with Lewis Mumford (edited by Robert Spiller), Brooks was even more scornful in his dismissal of Sinclair.

The fact is that Brooks was attacking an approach to writing that many later writers have continued to use. John Steinbeck, for example, went to live with his characters for *Cannery Row*

(1945) and *The Grapes of Wrath* (1939). Still, detachment is important and Sinclair does lack it.

Kazin: "Powerful." By 1942, a critic of a later generation could be more dispassionate than Brooks in his appraisal of Sinclair. *The Jungle*, Alfred Kazin said in his classic *On Native Grounds*, is "the most powerful of all the muckraking novels . . . above all the story of the betrayal of youth by the America it had greeted so eagerly. . . . Here . . . was the great news story of the decade. . . . Sinclair had proved himself one of the great reporters of the Progressive era . . . ." Sinclair himself could not be unhappy with that description; Kazin comes closer to seeing Sinclair's real aims than Brooks does.

Swados' answer. In 1961, writing about *The Jungle* in the *Atlantic Monthly* (a piece later included in his book *A Radical's America*), Harvey Swados posed the question "why [do] we persist in reading this book?" The answer, he found, "is the furious passion with which Upton Sinclair . . . apotheosizes the sweat and agony of an essential generation of Americans, an entire generation without which this country could not possibly have achieved what it has." In partial answer to Brooks, Swados adds: "If he had done nothing more, Sinclair would have justified — as one way of functioning — the method not of immolation in the working class but of observation and creation." Like Zola, Sinclair had gone "notebook in hand, to research a new territory, and then retired to write, not in tranquillity but in the heat of anger and hope about the price paid by countless thousands to build what is known as a civilization. Zola's brutalized coal miners of northern France [*Germinal*] and Sinclair's immigrants of Chicago's Packingtown can nevermore be fully forgotten." Swados was able to take the weaknesses with the strengths: "When I came to reread *The Jungle* I found . . . I had forgotten quite completely the lengthy propagandistic passages . . . but that I had retained from boyhood an ineradicable memory of the wretchedness of the residents of Packingtown and of the horrors of the industry in which they slaved."

Bloodworth's summing up. By the 1970s, Sinclair's *The Jungle* had long regained its eminence in America, enjoying the same prestige at home as abroad: prestige as an American classic. The year 1975 alone saw two important book-length studies of Sinclair's life and works: Leon Harris' *Upton Sinclair: American Rebel* and Jon Yoder's *Upton Sinclair*. And in 1977 William A. Bloodworth, Jr., gave us a calm summing up of the value of *The Jungle* in his *Upton Sinclair*:

> As a literary work and a historical document . . . *The Jungle* demands attention primarily as a flawed but strenuous effort to depict a kind of life that had found little previous expression in American writing. Sinclair had no tradition and few models to follow.
>
> Inspired by his recent knowledge of Socialism, his personal commitment to the movement, and his first-hand observations of working-class existence, he broke new literary ground. His tools of perception were not always sharp, and at times he dug furiously rather than carefully, but . . . few readers — and not very many American writers — could ignore what he had done.

These later critics have probably given us the best explanation for Sinclair's original popularity, his survival of Big Business counterattacks, and his persistent popularity today. True, his "strenuous effort" had so worn him out that he could compose only a tired, thin conclusion to *The Jungle*. Still he had already, in the more memorable portion of the book, communicated to us his "furious passion" about a great, historic social injustice. In so doing, he reaffirmed social indignation as a legitimate inspiration for fiction in America.

Essay Questions and Model Answers

1. *In what ways is* The Jungle *regarded as part of the muckraking movement in American history? To what extent does the novel's "muckraking" explain its immediate and long-range success?*

ANSWER. *The Jungle* actually originated as a muckraking project and was frankly offered as such both in the version serialized in the Socialist *Appeal* (1905) and in the commercial book edition (1906).

Muckrakers were a group of writers who investigated abuses in business and politics and reported their findings usually in nonfiction but sometimes in fiction. Some of their best work appeared in magazines, like Charles E. Russell's articles on the Beef Trust, which ran in *Everybody's* (1905). They also produced best-selling books like Lincoln Steffens' *The Shame of the Cities* (1904) and Ida Tarbell's *The History of the Standard Oil Company* (1904).

They were dubbed "muckrakers" by President Theodore Roosevelt. He likened them to a character in Bunyan's *Pilgrim's Progress* who looks only downward as he uses his muckrake to "rake to himself the filth of the floor." While agreeing that many of their charges were true, Roosevelt complained that their methods were sensational and irresponsible. The movement would become so powerful that by 1912

Big Business would squash it by threatening to withdraw all advertising from magazines that ran muckraking articles.

After Sinclair's Civil War novel *Manassas* appeared (1904), the editor of the *Appeal* commissioned Sinclair to do for "wage slavery" what he had done for "chattel slavery." Sinclair spent seven weeks investigating the life of the "wage slaves" of the Beef Trust in Chicago and interviewing people in various professions — doctors, lawyers, politicians, real-estate men. He discovered that adults and children were forced to work at a furious pace, eleven or more hours per day, in unhealthful conditions, under the artificial stimulus of a "speed-up" system. Employers assumed no real responsibility for injuries suffered on dangerous jobs. Female employees were sexually harassed by bosses. When workers organized to seek redress of their grievances, their union was infiltrated by labor spies; when they went out on strike, the packers used illegal methods to break the strike.

So far as the general public was concerned, even more sensational were Sinclair's discoveries about the condition of the meat sold by the Beef Trust. Packers canned diseased meat and even carrion, swept refuse and even rats into the meat vats, and duped or bribed U.S. inspectors ostensibly on duty to prevent such practices.

Bribing in the plants was part of a vast system of graft and corruption that ruled Chicago. Illiterate immigrants were prematurely naturalized, through their employers' influence, and paid to vote as directed by their bosses. Public works were under "boss rule"; police, packers, and organized crime worked hand-in-hand, for example, to pressure women into prostitution.

So eager was Sinclair to stress the factual nature of his exposé that he used muckraking techniques even in writing his novel. Whole passages read like magazine nonfiction, and at one point, he even documents a passage with a long footnote quoting a government regulation!

Like other muckrakers, Sinclair enjoyed an immediate impact on American life. During serialization of *The Jungle*, more than a hundred letters demanding action reached the White House each day. The press treated the novel as political news. Roosevelt sent two commissions to validate Sinclair's charges and then pressured Congress to pass, in 1906, the Pure Food and Drug Act and a new Meat Inspection Act.

There is no doubt that the sensational sociopolitical content of *The Jungle* was at least as important as its literary value in making it a bestseller on both sides of the Atlantic. Today, *The Jungle* is regarded as one of the few works of fiction to leave its stamp on political as well as on literary history, ranking in this respect with Harriet Beecher Stowe's *Uncle Tom's Cabin* and Ivan Turgenev's *A Sportsman's Notebook*.

2. *How does* The Jungle *illustrate the difference, in literary theory, between "plot" and "story"?*

ANSWER. In the theory of fiction writing, *story* is the chronological order in which the events must have occurred; *plot* is the nonchronological order in which the author reveals those events. We can illustrate this by first reviewing the basic *story* Sinclair had in mind for *The Jungle* and the *plot* he designed to unfold that story.

Chronologically, the story is as follows: Until 1900, Jurgis Rudkus, his father Antanas, his fiancée Ona, her stepmother Elzbieta, and her family live in the Lithuanian forest. They eat natural foods, work out-of-doors, live in sturdy cabins, enjoy communal village life, but are oppressed and cheated by officials and the upper class. Into Lithuania come men from Chicago telling them that high-paying jobs await them there: in America everyone is equal and can do as he pleases. They hear, too, that one man of their village has struck it rich in Chicago. So the two families take their life savings and emigrate to America. In New York they are cheated by immigration officials; in Chicago they find their villager in debt. The rooming house he takes them to is filthy, overcrowded. But Jurgis, impressed by American technology, believes that if he works hard and does as he is told, he will be rewarded with security for his family.

Jurgis, his father, Elzbieta's brother, Ona's cousin Marija all get jobs in Packingtown, sign a mortgage for a "new" house, and happily plan for the wedding of Jurgis and Ona.

But soon they learn first-hand about dangerous working conditions in the plants, the packing of condemned meat, graft that pervades industry and politics. They find they've been conned by a real estate agent who sells old houses as new and conceals the real costs so that buyers will fail to meet the mortgage and so be dispossessed. They send Ona and even Elzbieta's children out to work. Jurgis and Ona start off married life deeply in debt.

Antanas dies from despair and cruel working conditions, and the youngest child from contaminated food. Jurgis drifts into the most hazardous and humiliating work — in a fertilizer plant. After she bears a son, Ona is forced into illicit sex by her boss; Jurgis attacks the man and is jailed; they lose their jobs and also their house.

After Ona dies in childbirth and Jurgis' son drowns in a puddle, Jurgis takes to drifting, now a tramp, now a migratory worker. Panhandling, he accidentally gets a hundred-dollar bill; cheated out of it by a bartender, he fights back and is jailed again.

Disillusioned with law and order, Jurgis drifts into the underworld, becoming a mugger, a hireling of corrupt politicians, then a strikebreaker. He is now financially secure, but meeting Ona's boss, he assaults him and is arrested. Back to begging, he discovers that Marija supports the survivors of the family through prostitution. Stumbling into a Socialist meeting, he hears a speech that sums up working-class life as he knows it. He becomes a Socialist, striving, through democratic means, for a society in which industry would be owned not for private profit but by the people at large.

Now instead of recounting these events in the chronological order just given, Sinclair devises a nonchronological *plot*. He begins his novel *in medias res* (in the middle of things), with the wedding feast. This approach gives Sinclair the perfect opportunity to introduce most of his characters, their situations, and his main themes. Then, in Chapters 2 through 6, he uses a series of flashbacks to tell us the earlier history of the two families in Lithuania and America. In Chapter 7, he resumes the action where Chapter 1 left off. In Chapters 7 through 31 he uses continuous action with occasional flashbacks, like Ona's telling Jurgis how her illicit relation with her boss had begun months before.

Sinclair's rearrangement of events thus provides a good example of the difference between *story* and *plot*. From the author's point of view, *plot* is a mechanism for unfolding a *story* in a suspenseful, dramatic manner. From the reader's point of view, *plot* is the means by which he enjoys piecing together the whole *story*.

3. *To what extent can Sinclair be called a Zolaist?*

ANSWER. The nineteenth-century French novelist Emile Zola believed that the Darwinian Theory showed the novelist how to develop his art as a science. The novelist must study his characters as products, as resultants, of the forces of heredity and environment. He must approach his material with scientific objectivity, scrap all preconceptions, sentiment, and moral judgment, simply observe and record data: not selected data but all data, no matter how disgusting, "impolite," or "unliterary" they might seem. The novelist must also scrap the *traditional* plot, which to Zola is a deliberate distortion of the facts of life to produce a predetermined moral result — as when stories end with virtue rewarded and evil punished. Instead of designing such an artificial plot, the Zolaist stresses the chain of causation: each link in his action is logically connected to previous circumstances. Thus human feelings, victory, fate, everything appears as the inevitable workings-out of the laws of Nature. Hence Zolaism is commonly called naturalism.

From Darwin, Zola derived three specific lessons: (1) The novelist must study the effects that a *change of environment* has on his characters. (2) He must allow chance, accident, luck, coincidence to play their "natural" role in his action as they do in evolution itself. (3) He must study the *techniques of survival* in his characters' struggle for existence.

Zola's approach usually creates characters who are simply the end products of circumstances. A naturalistic character does not seem to grow so much as become aware how he is trapped by situations historical, economic, and natural. For example, falling in love and getting married, a person is trapped by Nature's drive to reproduce. He can thus become a victim, say, of unscrupulous businessmen who exploit his need to support his family.

Upton Sinclair was a Zolaist only so far as it served his needs as a Socialist writer. As Zola required, Sinclair filled notebooks with exhaustive data on the life and work, the cultural and family background, of his characters, his immigrant laborers. He uses the effects of their change of environment, from European forest to Chicago slum, as one of his main subjects.

In the Old World, for example, Elzbieta's family ate natural food, lived in solid houses, and worked in healthful surroundings. In Chicago, they eat contaminated food, live in shoddy housing, work in unhealthful places. They left Lithuania to escape oppression by the upper classes, only to discover in America new forms of oppression such as the "speed-up," systematic sexual harassment, discrimination against the poor by a "democratic" legal system. The reader can only conclude that a whole generation of immigrants has been lured out of a relatively secure and dignified life in Europe, only to be humiliated and sacrificed on the altar of "progress" in industrial America.

The effect of the change of environment is best symbolized in Sinclair's opening chapter. Jurgis' father and stepmother-in-law have expected that at the wedding feast revelers would follow the Lithuanian communal custom of contributing money not only to pay for the food, wine, and entertainment but also to give the newlyweds a "nest egg." Instead, the elders are shocked as the younger guests, adapting cynical American ways of "rugged individualism," eat, drink, dance, and then sneak out without paying. In America, then, Jurgis and Ona must begin married life heavily in debt.

In accordance with Zola's demand for the full truth, no matter how sordid, Sinclair describes the vermin in a rooming house, rats in the meat-packing plants, children scraping in the garbage dumps for food. Carefully he documents techniques: how schoolboys become newsboys, how a machine turns rods into bolts, how a politician rigs an election, how a prostitute budgets her income.

Finally, Sinclair makes clear how sheer luck — good or bad — influences life. Only because of an accident — streetcars were not running one wintry night — does Jurgis discover Ona's relations with Connor. And it is simple luck that the political meeting Jurgis seeks refuge in is run by Socialists.

However, Sinclair departs from Zolaism in several significant ways. He makes no pretense of objectivity: he is wholeheartedly on the side of the workers. He does not scrap his sentiments or his moral judgments: he is always present as the indignant, sarcastic, judgmental author. Further, he rescues his main character from the typical Zolaist fate. Jurgis' father, wife, son, and in-laws all go down to defeat as victims of circumstances, but Jurgis finally escapes the trap. True, one could argue that Jurgis' fate is still Zolaist since it is chance that leads him into a good (Socialist) environment, but Sinclair's ending is not truly Zolaist: *The Jungle* does not end in total defeat but in bright hope for a new world for everyone.

4. *Discuss Sinclair's treatment of minority groups in* The Jungle.

ANSWER. In the strict meaning of the term, a "minority" is a group of people who are easily discriminated against and exploited because they are different from, and less numerous than, the dominant population, or the majority. In this limited sense, we can consider how Sinclair treats four minorities: recent immigrants, the working poor, Jews, and blacks. But in the broadest sense, a minority is a group that, regardless of size, is allowed to play only *minor*, subordinate roles in society. In this larger sense, we can discuss how Sinclair treats a fifth "minority" — the less powerful half of the population, women under patriarchy.

As part of his muckraking, Sinclair exposes the way recent immigrants — like Jurgis, Antanas, Elzbieta — are exploited in Packingtown. Agents of the packers have lured them to America on false pretenses. They are not warned that the

American worker has not only higher wages but also higher costs, that his job is insecure, that he lives in slums and labors long hours in dangerous environments. They are lured to Chicago to provide a large number of workers who will have to compete among themselves for a much smaller number of jobs. In other words, those who do get jobs must all work at the lowest wage acceptable to the poorest among them.

Sinclair also treats of the way immigrants are victimized because they do not yet understand English. On arrival, Jurgis' party is cheated by immigration officials working hand-in-hand with hotel keepers. They are cheated by real-estate men who count on their inability to read legal documents. In *The Jungle* illiterate immigrants are lured en masse into voting the way their employers dictate.

Jurgis, Ona, Marija are part of a larger minority, "the working poor," whose plight Sinclair discusses in detail and in terms of economic theory. They are forced to overwork for rewards calculated according to the "Iron Law of Wages": they are paid just enough to meet their barest needs. They must do dangerous work at their own risk: there is no compensation for injuries and illnesses suffered from working conditions. Poor workers like Jurgis enjoy no equality before the law. Twice he tells the truth in court. Each time the judge decides in favor of Jurgis' accuser who lies but has economic power on his side. In short, Sinclair amply illustrates Engles' Law: The curse of the poor is their poverty. They are always kept off-balance, vulnerable, on the edge of disaster.

Jurgis finally realizes that "people who worked with their hands were a class apart, and were made to feel it." Near the end (Chapter 31), Schliemann examines the plight of the workers in Socialist terms — they are victims of greed fostered by the profit system — derived mainly from Edward Bellamy's *Looking Backward*. Earlier (Chapter 10), Sinclair uses a Bellamy argument to question American treatment of the poor: "They were willing to work . . . and when people did their best," ought they not to be rewarded? Indeed, very early in the book (Chapter 5), Tamozsius, also a Socialist, tells Jurgis that in America, honest work is not rewarded: "If you met a man who was rising . . . you met a knave."

It is in his exposé of corrupt government that Sinclair shows how prejudice against religious minorities is used by political bosses. Jurgis is hired to campaign, among his fellow workers, for Scotty Doyle and therefore against Scotty's opponent, a Jewish brewer. Jurgis is encouraged to use anti-Semitic arguments: "why did they want to vote for a 'sheeny'?"

Now Sinclair's account of anti-Semitic tactics in politics (Chapter 25) is well focused, so that we are sure the jibes at the "sheeny" are made by the politicians, not by Sinclair himself. Unfortunately, in other situations Sinclair is not so careful about establishing an artistic point of view. We realize that when Sinclair describes a scene through Jurgis' eyes yet uses literary allusions (to Homer, for example) that would never occur to Jurgis. It is Sinclair's own point of view that he blends in with Jurgis'. And unhappily, Sinclair again blurs the point of view when he treats attitudes toward Negroes during the meat cutters' strike (Chapter 26).

He reports how the packers recruit criminals as strikebreakers, and any recent immigrants or arrivals naive enough to be trapped. These include blacks imported from the South. Jurgis, once the dupe of Boss Scully's anti-Semitic tactics, now turns his prejudices on these allegedly "stupid black Negroes" who allegedly "did not want to work." In describing the racial tensions created by the strikebreaking — and fostered by the packers — Sinclair describes "young white girls . . . rubbing elbows with big buck Negroes."

Unfortunately, Sinclair here so confuses the point of view that we could again read these attitudes not as a character's but as the author's. Since Sinclair is obviously sympathetic to outcasts from society — like immigrant Lithuanians and despised workers — we cannot believe that Sinclair is himself racist. But it is sad that carelessness with artistic point of view creeps into his writing again at this point, where focus is so desirable.

Sinclair suffers no such lapses when he treats of the condition of women, mainly through his characterization of Ona and Ona's cousin Marija. Jurgis is convinced that he must "protect" Ona, that she is essentially inferior, that only one career should be open to her: housewifery and motherhood. Sinclair contrasts Ona's dependent status with Marija's independence: Marija goes out to work in the plants and ironically can command higher wages than Jurgis can! Sinclair portrays Jurgis as still feeling superior though, even toward Marija, because he is a man, and she a woman.

Two great crises in the book occur when Sinclair reveals how the economic system preys on women. When Jurgis is forced to send Ona out to work, she is forced to submit to her boss or see all her family fired. And Marija, at the beginning the defender of propriety, learns by the end that only impropriety pays off. The only reliable way she can support her family is through prostitution.

In representing the case for oppressed minorities, then, Sinclair — because of ineptitude in establishing artistic point of view — fails to be fair to the Black American. But he does give us an excellent picture of the plight of other victims of discrimination — the immigrant, the Jew, the poor worker, the woman.

Selected Bibliography

Basic research. The following lists of selected books and periodicals will meet the needs of students preparing research or critical papers on the college or high school level. Some works listed here contain bibliographies that provide additional leads.

Advanced research. Graduate students, professional scholars, teachers, and anyone else engaged in advanced research should also consult Ronald Gottesman, *Upton Sinclair: An Annotated Checklist* (Kent, Ohio: Kent State University Press, 1973). Ultimately, they must also investigate the Sinclair archives housed in the Lilly Library of Indiana University.

BOOKS

Bloodworth, William A., Jr. *Upton Sinclair*. Boston: Twayne Publishers, 1977.

Brooks, Van Wyck. *Emerson and Others*. New York: E. P. Dutton, 1927.

————*Sketches in Criticism*. New York: Dutton, 1932.

Cronon, E. David. *Twentieth Century America*. Volume I, 1909 to 1933. Homewood, Illinois: The Dorsey Press, 1965.

Dell, Floyd. *Upton Sinclair: A Study in Social Protest*. New York: Doubleday, Doran & Company, 1927.

Downs, Robert B. "Afterword." *The Jungle*. New York: The New American Library, 1963.

Evans, I.O. "Introduction." *An Upton Sinclair Anthology*. Newcastle: Northumberland Press, 1934.

Filler, Louis. *The Muckrakers: Crusaders for American Liberalism.* Chicago: Henry Regnery, 1968.

Harbaugh, William Henry. *Power and Responsibility: The Life and Times of Theodore Roosevelt.* New York: Farrar, Straus, and Cudahy, 1961.

Harris, Leon. *Upton Sinclair: American Rebel.* New York: Thomas Y. Crowell, 1975.

Josephson, Matthew. *The Robber Barons.* New York: Harcourt, Brace, & World, 1962.

Kazin, Alfred. *On Native Grounds: An Interpretation of American Prose Literature.* New York: Reynal & Hitchcock, 1942.

Parrington, V.L. *American Dreams: A Study of American Utopias.* Providence, R.I.: Brown University Press, 1947.

Rayback, Joseph G. *A History of American Labor.* New York: The Free Press, 1966.

Regier, C.C. *The Era of the Muckrakers.* Gloucester, Mass.: Peter Smith, 1957.

Rideout, Walter B. *The Radical Novel in the United States.* New York: Hill and Wang, 1956.

Root, Waverly, and Richard Rochemont. *Eating in America: A History.* New York: Thomas Y. Crowell, 1976.

Rubinstein, Annette T. *The Great Tradition in English Literature from Shakespeare to Shaw.* New York: The Citadel Press, 1953; New York: Modern Reader Paperback, 1969.

Sinclair, Mary Craig. *Southern Belle.* New York: Crown Publishers, 1957.

Sinclair, Upton. *American Outpost: A Book of Reminiscences.* New York: Farrar & Rinehart, 1932.

——*The Autobiography of Upton Sinclair.* New York: Harcourt, Brace & World, 1962.

——"Introduction to the Viking Press Edition, 1946." *The Jungle.* New York: Viking Press, 1946.

Spiller, Robert Ernest, editor. *The Van Wyck Brooks – Lewis Mumford Letters, 1921 – 1963.* New York: Dutton, 1970.

Sullivan, Mark. *Our Times.* Volume II, America Finding Herself. New York: Charles Scribner's Sons, 1926 – 1935.

Swados, Harvey. *A Radical's America.* Boston: Little, Brown and Company, 1962.

Van Doren, Carl. *Contemporary American Novelists, 1900 – 1920.* New York: Macmillan, 1927; revised edition, 1940.

Yoder, Jon. *Upton Sinclair.* New York: Ungar, 1975.

PERIODICALS

Anonymous. "Jurgis Rudkus and 'The Jungle.' A 'Dispassionate Examination' of Upton Sinclair's Application of Zola's Methods to a Chicago Environment." *The New York Times Book Review*, March 3, 1906.

——"Meat Inspection Bill Passes the Senate." *The New York Times*, May 26, 1906.

Appeal to Reason. Girard, Kansas: Appeal Publishing Co., September 17, 1904; February 25 to November 4, 1905.

Armour, J. Ogden. "The Packers and the People." *The Saturday Evening Post*, March 10, 1906.

Frankel, Max. "Johnson Welcomes Upton Sinclair, 89, at Meat Bill Signing." *The New York Times*, December 16, 1967.

New York Times, The. May 21, May 26 (see Anonymous), May 27, May 29, May 30, 1906.

New York Times Book Review, The. January 27, February 17, March 3 (see Anonymous), 1906.

One Hoss Philosophy. October 1905.

Sinclair, Upton. "Our Bourgeois Literature: The Reason and the Remedy." *Collier's*, October 8, 1904.

——"The Socialist Party: Its Aims in the Present Campaign." *Collier's*, October 29, 1904.

——"Stockyards Secrets." *Collier's*, March 24, 1906.

——"The Socialist Party." *World's Work*, April 1906.

——"The Condemned Meat Industry: A Reply to Mr. J. Ogden Armour." *Everybody's Magazine*, May 1906.

——"Is *The Jungle* True?" *Independent*, May 17, 1906.

Swados, Harvey. "The World of Upton Sinclair." *Atlantic Monthly*, December 1961.

REFERENCE BOOKS

N. W. Ayer and Son's American Newspaper Annual. Philadelphia: N. W. Ayer and Son, 1905, 1906.

Columbia Dictionary of Modern European Literature. Second edition. New York: Columbia University Press, 1980.

NOTES

NOTES

NOTES

NOTES

NOTES

NOTES

NOTES

NOTES

NOTES

NOTES

NOTES

MONARCH®
NOTES AND STUDY GUIDES

ARE AVAILABLE AT RETAIL STORES EVERYWHERE

In the event your local bookseller
cannot provide you with other
Monarch titles you want —

ORDER ON THE FORM BELOW:

Complete order form appears
on inside front & back covers
for your convenience.

Simply send retail price, local
sales tax, if any, plus 35¢ per
book to cover mailing and
handling.

TITLE #	AUTHOR & TITLE (exactly as shown on title listing)	PRICE
	PLUS ADDITIONAL 35¢ PER BOOK FOR POSTAGE	
	GRAND TOTAL	$

MONARCH® PRESS, a Simon & Schuster Division of Gulf & Western Corporation
Mail Service Department, 1230 Avenue of the Americas, New York, N.Y. 10020

I enclose $ .... to cover retail price, local sales tax, plus mailing
and handling.

Name _____
(Please print)
Address _____

City _____ State _____ Zip _____

Please send check or money order. We cannot be responsible for cash.